MANZANAR

Commentary by John Hersey

Photographs by Ansel Adams

MANZANAR

By John Armor and Peter Wright

VINTAGE BOOKS

A DIVISION OF RANDOM HOUSE
NEW YORK

to our parents

Contents

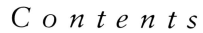

Acknowledgments

I would like to express my debt to the seminal research and writings on the evacuations by Roger Daniels in *The Politics of Prejudice* (Atheneum, 1968), *Concentration Camps U.S.A.* (Holt, Rinehart & Winston, 1972), and *The Decision to Relocate the Japanese Americans* (Lippincott, 1975); I should also like to thank Linda Amster, who dug up valuable material on General DeWitt.

John Hersey
Key West, Florida

WELCOME TO MANZANAR

Originally, Manzanar was only a dot on the map, a lonely cross-roads in Inyo County, California, near the rugged eastern Sierra. But in the spring of 1942, in only six weeks, Manzanar became a full-grown city of more than ten thousand people.

It was an unusual city. There were armed guards on towers with machine guns and searchlights, and barbed wire, and row upon row of barracks. But it was an American city, populated by American citizens, though only a handful of Manzanar's residents had come here voluntarily.

Manzanar, which means "apple orchard," was named by the Spanish, who were the first to explore this valley, in the eighteenth century. At one time it was a fertile place, but in 1919 the farms of the area were bought up by the government. The water they depended upon was diverted into the massive Los Angeles Aqueduct to serve that growing city, and as a result, the Owens Valley degenerated into a man-made desert.

On March 21, 1942, the first Japanese Americans arrived at Manzanar. That day, eighty-two people voluntarily entered the camp, when the military was only "requesting" such resettlement. Soon after, the rest were compelled to come. They came in military buses and vans, accompanied by armed guards who were either army soldiers or military police. Initially, a few came in a caravan of 240 cars, also under guard. Some were brought on trains.

Most of these Japanese Americans were from California, though some were from Oregon, Washington, and Hawaii. Officially, the government called them "evacuees." But these were not evacuees in the ordinary sense of being temporarily displaced, free to move on or go home when the emergency was over; the citizens of Manzanar were prisoners, plain and simple.

Half of the population were women. One-quarter were school-aged children. Some were infants, some elderly people barely able to walk. None had been charged with any crime, much less convicted of one, such as spying or sabotage; nor would any of them be, in the future. Yet the government claimed that these people were potential enemies of the United States.

The government also maintained that these people were brought to the camp "for their own protection," as it wrote in the explanatory booklet *Questions and Answers for Evacuees*. But, as one former prisoner observed forty-five years later, "If it was for our protection, why did the guns point inward, rather than outward?"

Living quarters consisted of 504 barracks. A family of four was officially allowed a space of twenty by twenty-five feet. There were steel-framed army cots, straw mattresses, and electricity. There were communal mess halls and laundry facilities. By October, 1942, the population had grown to 10,271, slightly more than the camp's intended capacity.

M R. AND MRS. RICHARD IZUMO
AND CHILDREN

Conditions at Manzanar were harsh. Even in the late spring, the nighttime temperatures in the valley dropped to freezing. In summer, temperatures often rose above 110 degrees. Despite the climate, the prisoners were required to grow their own food. Creating farms required a diversion of water to irrigate the fields. But most of the land remained barren. As one former prisoner described it, "The main thing you remembered was the dust, always the dust."

There were only two ways to leave Manzanar. One was by joining the armed forces. Many Japanese Americans from this camp, and the other nine camps like it, did so, once they were permitted to. Many of them lie buried in foreign lands as a result of their service to their country.

Later on, others were allowed to leave in order to practice their skills and professions as a contribution to the war effort. But to do so, many were compelled to go east. Both the exclusionary laws and deep prejudice prevented them from returning to the western States where they had been born and raised.

Children were born here. Old people died here. Most prisoners spent as long as three and a half years at Manzanar. Then, in September 1945, almost as quickly as it had come into being, the camp closed. Its remaining prisoners were set free.

In 1943, a man who would later be known as one of the world's greatest photographers visited Manzanar at the request of camp director Ralph Merritt, and took photographs of the people and circumstances there. It was the only time in his long career that he made

*Construction of the Manzanar Cemetery
Monument was completed earlier than
expected and dedicated Saturday
afternoon. Directed by R. F. Kado,
landscape supervisor, approximately 60
members of the Buddhist Young People's
organization voluntarily assisted in the
construction together with Block 9
residents.*

*[The inscription on this monument
(opposite) reads, "Memorial to the Dead."
Because of a lack of money and access to
materials, most graves at Manzanar did
not have monuments. This memorial was
for all who were buried there.]*
AUGUST 18, 1943 MANZANAR FREE PRESS

what he called a "photo essay"—what we now call a documentary. His name was Ansel Adams.

Today, nothing remains at Manzanar but a graveyard with a single bold monument; nothing remains *of* it but the memories of those who were detained there, some documents, some photographs, and a quest for justice as yet denied.

MONUMENT IN CEMETERY

THE PHOTOGRAPHERS OF MANZANAR

Ansel Adams was a friend of Manzanar's second director, Ralph Merritt, who was familiar with Adams's work as a photographer in Yosemite National Park, not far from the camp. It was he who invited Adams to Manzanar, and to make a photographic record of it.

Adams described his reasons for accepting this assignment in the introduction to his book about Manzanar, *Born Free and Equal*:

> Moved by the human story unfolding in the encirclement of desert and mountains, and by the wish to identify my photography . . . with the tragic momentum of the times, I came to Manzanar with my cameras in the fall of 1943. . . . I believe that the arid splendor of the desert, ringed with towering mountains, has strengthened the spirit of the people of Manzanar. I do not say all are conscious of this influence, but I am sure most have responded, in one way or another, to the resonances of their environment. From the harsh soil they have extracted fine crops; they have made gardens glow in the firebreaks and between the barracks. Out of the jostling, dusty confusion of the first bleak days in raw barracks they have modulated to a democratic internal society and a praiseworthy personal adjustment to conditions beyond their control.

VALLEY, MOUNTAINS, AND BARBED WIRE

Adams published *Born Free and Equal* in 1944. Secretary of the Interior Harold Ickes contributed the book's foreword, since by then the camps were under his jurisdiction. Secretary Ickes and Attorney General Francis Biddle were the only cabinet-level officials in the administration to make it clear that they thought the internments were wrong. Secretary Ickes sought to end them as soon as possible. He even sent two copies of *Born Free and Equal* to President Roosevelt, with a personal note.

The words and pictures in that book did not convey a welcome message to much of the uneasy American public in 1944. Copies were publicly burned in protest, making *Born Free and Equal* a rare book today.

Adams did not renew the copyright on his book. At the same time, he gave the Library of Congress the negatives and prints of his work at Manzanar, in hopes that the full story would eventually—perhaps at a more objective time—reach most of the American people.

Because of Director Merritt's enlightened administration, a greater photographic record exists of life at Manzanar than at any of the other internment camps. In addition to Adams, Dorothea Lange, *Life* magazine photographers, and many newspaper and wire-service photographers from the outside visited Manzanar during the camp's operation. But the camp also had a resident photographer.

Toyo Miyatake was a professional photographer in Los Angeles when the evacuation order for his area forced him to move with his family into Manzanar. He was able to store his photographic equipment, but not to bring it into the camp. At the time, by military orders,

"Japanese" were forbidden even to own cameras. However, Miyatake smuggled a lens and shutter into the camp. With those he built a wooden camera, and began to take pictures.

When Director Merritt found out, he could have arrested him for the "crime" of being Japanese and taking pictures. Instead, he allowed Miyatake to send for the rest of his equipment and supplies and to continue his work. Under regulations, Miyatake could, for a time, only load and set the camera; a Caucasian had to trip the shutter. Eventually that restriction was lifted too. Miyatake's photographs of Manzanar are excellent, and were even once exhibited side by side with Adams's.

Restrictions existed even for visiting photographers, including Adams: they were forbidden to photograph the guard towers, the guards, or the barbed wire. Yet Adams worked all three into his images. *City in the Desert* (page xix) implies the existence of the guard towers, because it was taken from one. *Valley, Mountains, and Barbed Wire* (page xvi) at first glance looks like a pastoral scene; on closer inspection, barbed wire emerges from the hedgerow across the center of the picture. And the presence of guards is suggested in *Welcome to Manzanar* (page x) by the sign at the left of the photograph, which reads, STOP. MILITARY POLICE.

ADAMS PHOTO EXHIBIT,
MANZANAR MUSEUM

LOCAL PHOTOS ON DISPLAY

Since Monday, an exhibit of photographs of Manzanar, taken by Ansel Adams, noted photographer, has been on display in the Visual Education Museum, 8-15, announced Kiyotsugu Tsuehiyo, director of the Museum.

This exhibit, which is slated to last about a week, will include approximately 80 photographs of this camp.
JANUARY 26, 1944 MANZANAR FREE PRESS

"A Mistake of Terrifically Horrible Proportions"

By John Hersey

閒
遍

MESS LINE: NOON AT MANZANAR

On March 31, 1942, there appeared on notice boards in certain communities on the western seaboard of the United States a number of broadsides bearing the ominous title "Civilian Exclusion Order." These bulletins warned all residents of Japanese descent that they were going to have to move out of their homes. No mention was made of where they would have to go. Heads of families were directed to report for instructions at neighboring "control stations."

The Japanese attack on Pearl Harbor had taken place a little less than four months earlier. These Exclusion Orders cast a wide net. There were about 125,000 persons of Japanese ancestry scattered along the coastal tier of states then, and seven out of ten of them, having been born there, were full-fledged citizens of the United States, yet no distinction between alien and native was made among those summoned to control stations. The United States was at war with Germany and Italy as well as with Japan, but no German or Italian enemy aliens, to say nothing of German Americans or Italian Americans, were subjected to these blanket Exclusion Orders. Only "Japanese aliens and non-aliens," as the official euphemism put it.

Each person who responded to the summons to a control station had to register the names of all family members and was told to show up at a certain time and place, a few days later, with all of them, bringing along only such baggage as they could carry by hand—for a trip to a destination unknown. Names had become numbers. "Henry went to the control station to register the family," wrote a Japanese American woman, years later. "He came home with twenty tags, all numbered 10710, tags to be attached to each piece of baggage, and one to hang from our coat lapels. From then on, we were known as family #10710." "I lost my identity," another woman would assert, describing the replacement of her name by a number. "I lost my privacy and dignity."

There followed a period of devastating uncertainty and anxiety. "We were given eight days to liquidate our possessions," one of the evacuees testified at an investigation by the Department of Justice, many years later. The time allowed varied from place to place. "We had about two weeks," another recalled, "to do something. Either lease the property or sell everything." Another: "While in Modesto, the final notice for evacuation came with a four-day notice." Under the circumstances, the evacuees had to dispose of their businesses, their homes, and their personal possessions at panic prices to hostile buyers.

"It is difficult," one man would later testify, "to describe the feeling of despair and humiliation experienced by all of us as we watched the Caucasians coming to look over our possessions and offering such nominal amounts, knowing we had no recourse but to accept whatever they were offering because we did not know what the future held for us." One woman, with three days' time to make a

BURNING LEAVES, AUTUMN DAWN

decision, sold a twenty-six-room hotel for $500. A man who owned a pickup truck and had just bought a set of new tires and a new battery for $125, asked only that amount of a prospective buyer. "The man 'bought' our pickup for $25." One homeowner, in despair, wanted to burn his house down. "I went to the storage shed to get the gasoline tank and pour the gasoline on my house, but my wife . . . said, 'Don't do it, maybe somebody can use this house; we are civilized people, not savages.' "

By far the greatest number of Nisei (the term for first-generation Japanese Americans that came to be used as the generic word for all ethnic Japanese living in America) were in agriculture, raising fruit, truck vegetables, nursery plants, and specialty crops. They had worked wonders in the soil. They owned about one-fiftieth of the arable land in the three coast states, and what they had made of their farms is suggested by the fact that the average value per acre of all farms in the three states in 1940 was $37.94, while an acre on a Nisei farm was worth, on average, $279.96. But now the farmers had to clear out in a matter of days. The Mother's Day crop of flowers, the richest harvest of the year, was about to be gathered; it had to be abandoned. An owner of one of the largest nurseries in southern California, unable to dispose of his stock, gave it all to the veteran's hospital adjoining his land. A strawberry grower asked for a deferral of his evacuation summons for a few days, so that he could harvest his crop. Denied the permission, he bitterly plowed the berries under. The next day the FBI charged him with an act of sabotage and put him in jail.

Assured by authorities that they could store property and reclaim it after the war, many put their chattels in impromptu warehouses—homes and garages and outbuildings—only to have the stored goods, before long, vandalized or stolen. Some leased their property but never received rents. Some were cheated by their tenants, who sold the property as if it were their own. Promised that their cars would be stored by the Federal Reserve Bank, the evacuees turned over nearly two thousand of them. Many later took the offer of the army to buy their cars at token prices; those who chose not to sell were notified in the late fall of 1942 that their cars had been requisitioned willy-nilly by the army, "in consideration of national interest in wartime."

On the day of departure, evacuees found themselves herded into groups of about five hundred, mostly at railroad and bus stations. They wore numbered tags and carried hand baggage containing possessions they had packed in fear and perplexity, not knowing where they were going. They embarked on buses and trains. Some trains had blacked-out windows. Uniformed guards carrying weapons patrolled the cars. "To this day," one woman recalled long afterward, "I can remember vividly the plight of the elderly, some on stretchers, orphans herded onto the train by caretakers, and especially a young couple with four preschool children. The mother had two frightened toddlers hanging on to her coat. In her arms she carried two crying babies. The father had diapers and other baby paraphernalia strapped to his back. In his hands he struggled with duffel bag and suitcase."

Each group was unloaded, after its trip, at one of sixteen assembly centers, most of which were located at fairgrounds and racetracks. There, seeing barbed wire and searchlights, and under the guard of

YUCHI HARATA

"A Mistake of Terrifically Horrible Proportions"

guns, these "aliens and non-aliens" were forced to realize that all among them—even those who had sons or brothers in the United States Army—were considered to be dangerous people. At the entrance to the Tanforan assembly center, one man later remembered, "stood two lines of troops with rifles and fixed bayonets pointed at the evacuees as they walked between the soldiers to the prison compound. Overwhelmed with bitterness and blind with rage, I screamed every obscenity I knew at the armed guards, daring them to shoot me." Most were silent, dazed. Many wept.

A typical assembly center was located at the Santa Anita racetrack. The stables for the racehorses had been whitewashed. Each family was allotted a space in the horse stalls of about two hundred square feet, furnished with cots, blankets, and pillows; the evacuees had to make their own pallets, filling mattress shells with straw. There were three large mess halls, in which shifts of two thousand each stood in line with tin plates and cups, to be served mass-cooked food that cost an average of thirty-nine cents per person per day—rough fare, usually overcooked, such as brined liver, which, one testified, "would bounce if dropped." "We lined up," another later wrote, "for mail, for checks, for meals, for showers, for washrooms, for laundry tubs, for toilets. . . . " Medical care, under jurisdiction of the Public Health Service, was provided by evacuee doctors and nurses, who were recruited to serve their fellow inmates in an improvised clinic, supplied at first with nothing more than mineral oil, iodine, aspirin, sulfa ointment, Kaopectate, and alcohol. Toilets were communal, without compartments. The evacuees bathed in what had been horse showers, with a partition between the men's and the women's sections. When the

women complained that men were climbing the partition and looking at them, a camp official responded, "Are you sure you women are not climbing the walls to look at the men?"

Toward the end of May 1942, evacuees began to be transferred from these temporary assembly centers to thirteen permanent concentration camps—generally called by the more decorous name of "relocation centers"—where they would be held prisoner until a few months before the end of the war. By November 1, 106,770 internees had been put behind barbed wire in centers in six western states and Arkansas.

Thus began the bitterest national shame of the Second World War for the sweet land of liberty: the mass incarceration, on racial grounds alone, on false evidence of military necessity, and in contempt of their supposedly inalienable rights, of an entire class of American citizens —along with others who were not citizens in the country of their choice only because that country had long denied people of their race the right to naturalize. "My mother, two sisters, niece, nephew, and I left," one recalled in later years, "by train. Father joined us later. Brother left by bus. We took whatever we could carry. So much we left behind, but the most valuable thing I lost was my freedom."

This book gives us a record, in photographs whose clarity and beauty and truthfulness burn one's eyes, of the sad yet amazingly vivid half-life that was lived for so long in those final camps by American citizens and their alien kin, ripped on short notice from their homes and livelihoods, from their liberty and their pursuit of happiness. The

HIGH SCHOOL RECESS PERIOD

camp pictured here is the one that was quickly built to entrap evacuees at Manzanar, in the desert country of east central California. It happened in the passage of time that the Manzanar camp's second director, a humane and far-sighted man named Ralph Merritt, realized that history ought to have some testimony of what its victims had managed to salvage from an unprecedented American social crime. He had seen the consummate artistry of photographs taken in nearby Yosemite National Park by a friend of his, Ansel Adams, and he invited the great photographer to come to the camp to capture its woes and its marvels on film.

"Moved," Adams would later write, "by the human story unfolding in the encirclement of desert and mountains, and by the wish to identify my photography . . . with the tragic momentum of the times, I came to Manzanar with my cameras in the fall of 1943." He published his witnessing the next year, in a book titled *Born Free and Equal.* But the time was not ripe for such honesty. The war with Japan was not yet over, and the book's implicit message of guilt and shame did not go down well with a public still hungry for the unconditional surrender of a tenacious enemy. Copies of the book were actually burned in public ceremonies. The book hid itself away in the rare-book rooms of libraries and on microfilm. Adams eventually declined to renew the copyright on it and gave the negatives and prints of his photographs to the Library of Congress. Here again, at last, are some of them, to restore new energy to the sorry record—and to remind us that this very word *record,* in its ancient origins, meant "to bring back the heart."

But first it seems appropriate to re-engage the mind, for the stories of Manzanar and the other camps raise grave questions for the American polity: Could such a thing occur again? How did this slippage in the most precious traditions of a free country come about? Does the Bill of Rights provide a sufficient prophylactic against hysteria and bigotry in a time of national stress? Could the racism underlying these events some day reassert itself? Against the same race? Against another? What happened? What went wrong?

The Japanese attack on Pearl Harbor on December 7, 1941, threw the American psyche into a state of shock. For years there had been a mind-set in the United States about Japan that was suddenly proved to have been dangerously complacent and madly deluded. Americans had kept telling themselves that the Japanese were technological primitives; all they could do, the mythology held, was to copy American blueprints—and then go wrong in the making. Their warships turned turtle, it was said, as soon as they went down the ways. Despite four years' demonstration of the skill and dispatch—and cruelty—of the Japanese invasion of China, American military commanders in the Philippines and elsewhere issued boastful statements, over and over again, about how quickly the Japs, as they were scornfully called, would be wiped out if they dared attack American installations.

Then suddenly, within hours, the United States Pacific fleet was crippled at anchor. The United States air arm in the Philippines was wrecked on the ground. American pride dissolved overnight into

Clockwise from top left: FRANK NOBUO HOROSAWA, RUBBER CHEMIST; TOM KOBAYASHI; CATHERINE NATSUKO YAMAGUCHI, RED CROSS INSTRUCTOR; YOSHI MURAMOTO; MICHIKO SUGAWARA, STENOGRAPHER.

American rage and hysteria—and nowhere so disastrously as on the country's western shores.

On the seventh and eighth of December, President Franklin D. Roosevelt promptly proclaimed, and Congress voted, a state of war against Japan, and within days the other Axis powers, Germany and Italy, declared war on the United States. The President issued orders classifying nationals of those countries as enemy aliens. These orders gave responsibility for carrying out certain restrictions against enemy aliens of all three countries to Attorney General Francis Biddle and the Department of Justice. Biddle was given authority to establish prohibited zones, from which enemy aliens could be moved at will; to seize as contraband any weapons and other articles as required for national security; to freeze enemy aliens' funds; and to intern any of them who might be deemed dangerous. These were perfectly normal wartime precautions against enemy aliens only, for which there had been statutory precedent under President Woodrow Wilson in the First World War.

With great speed and efficiency, beginning on the very night of the attack, the Justice Department arrested certain marked enemy aliens of all three belligerent nations. Within three days, 857 Germans, 147 Italians, and 1,291 Japanese (367 of them in the Hawaiian Islands, 924 on the continent) had been rounded up. The arrests were made on the basis of remarkably thorough—though in some cases inaccurate—prior information that had been compiled by the Federal Bureau of Investigation, the Office of Naval Intelligence, and the Mil-

LOUISE TAMI NAKAMURA

itary Intelligence Service. With respect to the Japanese, it was evidently of enormous help that United States cryptologists had, a year earlier, in an initiative called Magic, broken all the Japanese diplomatic codes and ciphers. Intercepted Magic messages had designated certain Japanese patriotic organizations in the United States as potential sources of intelligence for the enemy, and many of the Japanese aliens arrested in the first sweeps were leaders of those groups.

On the night of December 8, when Pearl Harbor jitters were at their highest pitch, San Francisco suffered a false alarm of an air incursion. Military and/or naval radio trackers reported that enemy aircraft were soaring in over the Bay area and, later, that they had turned back to sea without attacking. Planes of the Second Interceptor Command took off from Portland and searched as far as six hundred miles offshore for a (nonexistent) Japanese aircraft carrier, from which the (phantom) enemy planes were assumed to have been launched. At the first alarm, sirens sounded a warning, and San Francisco was supposed to be blacked out at once, but skyscrapers blazed, neon lights winked at hundreds of night spots, and Alcatraz was like a heap of sparkling diamonds in the Bay.

Enter, the next morning, to center stage, a military figure in a high state of excitation. As commanding officer of the Fourth Army and Western Defense Command, Lt. Gen. John L. DeWitt was charged with making sure that there would be no Pearl Harbors on the West Coast. That morning he called a meeting at City Hall of Mayor Angelo Rossi and two hundred of the city's civic and business leaders, and, as *Life* would put it, he "almost spit with rage."

"You people," he said to them, "do not seem to realize that we are at war. So get this: Last night there were planes over this community. They were enemy planes. I mean Japanese planes. And they were tracked out to sea. You think it was a hoax? It is damned nonsense for sensible people to think that the Army and Navy would practice such a hoax on San Francisco." According to a reporter for *The New York Times,* General DeWitt's voice rose to a shout as he accused his hearers of "criminal, shameful apathy" in failing to black the city out. "Remember," he said, "that we're fighting the Japanese, who don't respect the laws of war. They're gangsters, and they must be treated as such." Then he shouted that it might have been "a good thing" if some bombs *had* been dropped. "It might have awakened some of the fools in this community who refuse to realize that this is a war."

On the night of this "air attack," one of General DeWitt's subordinates, Maj. Gen. Joseph W. Stilwell, later to be the famous "Vinegar Joe" of the doomed campaigns in Burma and China, wrote in pencil in a dime-store notebook that he used as a diary, "Fourth Army"—obviously meaning its headquarters—"kind of jittery." Two nights later, General DeWitt and his staff, hearing that there was to be an armed uprising of twenty thousand Nisei in the San Francisco area, whipped up a plan to put all of them in military custody—a plan fortunately aborted by the local FBI chief of station, Nat Pieper, who told the army that the "reliable source" for their news of the uprising was a flake whom Pieper had once employed and had had to fire because of his "wild imaginings." (There were, anyway, not quite

MITSU NAKAI AND BABY

twenty thousand Japanese-descended men, women, and children in the entire Bay area.) Next, on the twelfth, came "reliable information" that an enemy attack on Los Angeles was imminent, and DeWitt's staff drafted a general alarm that insanely would have advised all civilians to leave the city. Fortunately it was never broadcast. That night, General Stilwell wrote in his notebook that General DeWitt was a "jackass."

John Lesesne DeWitt was born on January 9, 1880, as an army brat at Fort Sidney, built during the Indian wars in Nebraska; his father was an army doctor who had served in the Civil War. John L. and his two brothers would all eventually wind up in the army, and their younger sister would marry a soldier. During John L.'s boyhood, his parents were shifted about, as the prairie wars against the Indians played themselves out, to Fort Hancock in Texas, Fort Missoula in Montana, Fort Sully in the Dakotas. When John L. was sixteen, he was sent off to Princeton. He applied to West Point, but was turned down. On November 1, 1898, the United States having gone to war with Spain, he dropped out of college—never to return—to accept a lieutenancy in the Twentieth Infantry, and he was sent to the Philippines. From then until the First World War, he was posted back and forth between stateside and the Philippines; one has to assume that his later attitudes toward nonwhites were shaped by the Indian wars and his intermittent Philippines duty. In late 1917 he went to France as a quartermaster, serving behind the lines as a supply officer during the Aisne-Marne, Saint Mihiel, Meuse-Argonne, and Champagne-Marne battles. Between wars, he lived the dull life of army posts—

"A Mistake of Terrifically Horrible Proportions"

Washington, Georgia, Texas, the Philippines. Late in 1939 he was put in command of the Fourth Army and then of the Western Defense Command, with headquarters in San Francisco's Presidio. When, four days after Pearl Harbor, Chief of Staff George C. Marshall designated the West Coast and Alaska a "theater of operations," making it a war zone, General DeWitt became—at least, it seemed, in his own eyes—the virtual dictator of the entire area.

The general tried to make it clear, in an interview not long after this, that he was in command both of troops and of civilians:

> Because our country hasn't been invaded since the Villa raid into Columbus, New Mexico, in 1916, our people are not war-wise as the peoples of Europe and Asia are. So, although millions of us live in combat zones liable to air attack and invasion at any moment, most of us don't realize it. . . . What it boils down to is this: If, in a war, civilians try to run military affairs—well, that's just what the Japanese and the Germans want. The best way a civilian can help, especially in any sudden emergency, is to keep minding his own business, prevent confusion, and do what he's told without any grumbling or back-seat driving.

He had put the matter of the reach of his authority quite a bit less delicately on the morning after the "air raid" on San Francisco. A reporter for *Collier's* quoted him as having said, "If I can't knock the seriousness of this situation into you with words, we'll have to turn it over to the police to knock it into you with clubs."

The first week of the war brought news of one setback after another. The Japanese struck at Midway, Wake, the Philippines, Hong Kong, the Malay Peninsula, and Thailand. They sank the British battleship *Prince of Wales* and the battle cruiser *Repulse* in the South Pacific. On December 13 they captured Guam. The American dream of invulnerability had suddenly been replaced by a feeling that the Japanese could do just about anything they wanted to do—including landing at any point along General DeWitt's vast coastal command.

Two days after Pearl Harbor, Navy Secretary Frank Knox went to Hawaii to try to find out what had gone wrong there. President Roosevelt had brought Knox, a Republican, into his cabinet as a signal of a desirable nonpartisanship in dangerous times. Before becoming publisher of the *Chicago Daily News,* Knox had been general manager of the Hearst newspapers during their shrill racist blasts against Chinese and Japanese immigration on the West Coast. On December 15, he returned to the mainland from his scouting trip and called a press conference, at which he said, "I think the most effective Fifth Column work of the entire war was done in Hawaii, with the possible exception of Norway." He carried back to Washington this report of treachery by resident Japanese, "both from the shores and from the sampans," and his absurdly impracticable recommendation that all those with Japanese blood be evacuated from Oahu. His charges were quickly denied, in confidential reports, by J. Edgar Hoover of the FBI; by John Franklin Carter, a journalist whom Roosevelt had enlisted to give him intelligence reports; and, after a few days, by Lt. Gen. Delos Emmons, the newly appointed commanding officer in the Hawaiian

Islands. But Frank Knox's statement was never denied by the government (which, by the way, from Pearl Harbor to V-J Day, would record not a single case of sabotage by a Japanese alien or a Japanese American worse than the plowing under of strawberries). Nothing was done to calm the fears on the West Coast caused by the scare headlines on the Knox statement:

FIFTH COLUMN TREACHERY TOLD

FIFTH COLUMN PREPARED ATTACK

SECRETARY OF NAVY BLAMES 5TH COLUMN FOR ATTACK

In 1943, when General DeWitt would submit to the Secretary of War his *Final Report* on the removal of the Japanese from the West Coast, its very first assertion would be: "The evacuation was impelled by military necessity." This absolutely nonexistent "necessity" was in part an artificial creation of General DeWitt's own jittery headquarters, which kept leaking unfounded rumors as if they were facts. Sample headlines from the relatively sober *Los Angeles Times:*

JAP BOAT FLASHES MESSAGES ASHORE

MAP REVEALS JAP MENACE

CAPS ON JAPANESE TOMATO PLANTS POINT TO AIR BASE

In his *Final Report,* General DeWitt wrote, "There were hundreds of reports nightly of signal lights visible from the coast, and of intercepts of unidentified radio transmissions." Hoover of the FBI scornfully ridiculed the "hysteria and lack of judgment" of DeWitt's

Military Intelligence Division. In a memo he wrote: "There was no sense in the Army losing their heads at they did in the Booneville Dam affair, where the power lines were sabotaged by cattle scratching their backs on the wires, or the 'arrows of fire' near Seattle, which was only a farmer burning brush as he had done for years." An official of the Federal Communications Commission reported on the question of radio intercepts:

> I have never seen an organization that was so hopeless to cope with radio intelligence requirements. . . . The personnel is unskilled and untrained. . . . They know nothing about signal identification, wave propagation, and other technical subjects, so essential to radio intelligence procedure. . . . As a matter of fact, the Army air stations have been reported by the Signal Corps as Jap enemy stations.

Not one case of identifiable shore-to-ship signaling could be verified by the FCC. Stilwell wrote in his diary his opinion of DeWitt's G-2 intelligence unit: "The [Fourth] Army G-2 is just another amateur, like all the rest of the staff. RULE: The higher the headquarters, the more important is calm. Nothing is ever as bad as it seems at first."

Another example of "military necessity" that DeWitt gave in his *Final Report* was "the fact that for a period of several weeks following December 7th, substantially every ship leaving a West Coast port was attacked by an enemy submarine. This seemed conclusively to point to the existence of hostile shore-to-ship (submarine) communication." Here was another of DeWitt's wild exaggerations. Nine Japanese submarines were in fact assigned to waters off the West

Coast in the early weeks of the war, but only four of the nine subs ever took part in attacks on ships; of the scores of ships leaving coast ports, only two tankers and one freighter were sunk in December.

General DeWitt urged random spot raids on homes of ethnic Japanese to seize "subversive" weapons and cameras. Attorney General Biddle stipulated that raiders should follow the constitutional requirement of finding probable cause for arrest, but DeWitt argued that being of Japanese descent was in itself probable cause. He insisted on searches without warrants, even of the homes of citizens. In the first four months of the war, 2,592 guns of various kinds were seized; 199,000 rounds of ammunition; 1,652 sticks of dynamite; 1,458 radio receivers; 2,014 cameras. But these numbers meant very little, because many of these objects were picked up wholesale in two raids—on a licensed gun shop and in the warehouse of a legitimate general store owner. The Justice Department finally concluded from FBI reports: "We have not found a single machine gun, nor have we found any gun in any circumstances indicating that it was to be used in a manner helpful to our enemies. We have not found a single camera which we have reason to believe was for use in espionage."

As a further justification of his supposed "military necessity," General DeWitt cited "the existence of hundreds of Japanese organizations in California, Washington, Oregon, and Arizona which, prior to December 7, 1941, were actively engaged in advancing Japanese war aims." Among the examples he gave were the Hokubei Butoku Kai, or Military Virtue Society of North America, which taught Japanese boys fencing, jiujitsu, and sumo wrestling; the Japanese Association of Sacramento, which, on February 11, 1940, had sponsored "an Emperor worshipping ceremony" in honor of the 2,600th anniversary of the founding of Japan; and the Heimusha Kai, which had been organized in 1937 to support the Japanese war in China. (General DeWitt of course made no mention of the fact that for several years the United States had supported that war through government-approved sales of scrap steel, fuel, and other supplies to Japan.) Another organization that aroused suspicion was the Society of the Amur River, which had been founded much earlier in advocacy of Japanese settlement of Manchuria; inasmuch as the Japanese characters for the river also meant "Black Dragon," the elderly gents who led this organization were thought to be particularly sinister.

The mere fact of having Japanese blood and skin was, to General DeWitt, enough basis for suspicion—a paranoiac suspicion of (in his words) "some vast conspiracy." "Because of the ties of race, the intense feeling of filial piety, and the strong bonds of common tradition, this population presented a tightly-knit racial group." When he wrote in his *Final Report* of the way the ethnic Japanese population had been scattered through his Defense Command, he used the military term "deployed"—"in excess of 115,000 persons deployed along the Pacific Coast"—as if these farmers and merchants and house servants had been posted by plan, poised for attack. "Throughout the Santa Maria Valley in [Santa Barbara] County, every utility, air field, bridge, telephone and power line or other facility of importance was flanked by Japanese." He wrote with alarm about "557 male Japanese less than twenty-five years of age who entered West Coast ports from

Japan during 1941"—young American citizens who had been sent to Japan for an average of 5.2 years for part of their schooling. To him, these must surely have been a trained fifth column.

In a press conference, later, General DeWitt would say to the assembled newspapermen, as if this alone proved the military necessity he was trying to assert, "A Jap is a Jap."

Racism based on skin color has a long-standing claim on the mind of American whites—and on that of Californians in a particular way. The Naturalization Act of 1790 allowed the immigration and naturalization of "any alien, being a free white person." After the Civil War, this was amended to include "aliens of African nativity." This still left out all those of brown or yellow skin, who were allowed at first to arrive in the West but not to become citizens.

The Chinese were the earliest to immigrate from Asia. Many came after the Civil War to build railroads, and in 1869, when the ribbons of track finally spanned the continent, ten thousand Chinese were suddenly thrown out of work on an already weak labor market. The panic of 1870 was blamed on "cheap Mongolian labor." One night in 1871, twenty Chinese were shot and hanged in the small town of Los Angeles; bullies cut off "John Chinaman's" pigtails; Chinese were beaten in the streets. An Irish immigrant, Dennis Kearney, rallied the Workingman's Party with the slogan "The Chinese Must Go!" In 1882, President Chester Arthur signed a bill which excluded Chinese from immigrating for ten years; the law was renewed in 1892 for

MR. MATSUMOTO AND CHILDREN

another decade, and it was made "permanent" in 1902. The law was not revoked until 1943, when China was an ally in World War II.

Japan was opened to American commerce by Commodore Matthew Perry in 1853, and some subsequent ills of the Japanese economy led to a heavy outflow of Japanese peasants, after about 1885, first to Hawaii and then to California. By the end of the century there were nearly 25,000 Japanese in the United States, and in the next eight years 127,000 entered the country. Soon American workmen's groups were beginning to agitate against this new source of cheap labor, and when the shocking news came in 1905 that the Japanese navy had routed the Russian fleet, so that Japan was suddenly seen as a dangerous world power, a virulent racist campaign began. The respectable and conservative *San Francisco Chronicle* warned that the "inundation of Japanese" must be checked, or there would be a "complete orientalization of the Pacific Coast." Some *Chronicle* headlines:

BROWN ARTISANS STEAL BRAINS OF WHITES

JAPANESE A MENACE TO AMERICAN WOMEN

THE YELLOW PERIL—HOW JAPANESE CROWD OUT THE WHITE RACE

Labor organizations banded together to form the Asiatic Exclusion League, the Anti-Jap Laundry League, the Anti-Japanese League of Alameda County. From the speech of a leader of the Exclusion League: "An eternal law of nature has decreed that the white cannot assimilate the blood of another without corrupting the very springs of civilization." The League brought together the relatively moderate unions of the American Federation of Labor with the more radical

HANDS OF LATHE WORKER

left. "I am first of all a white man," the novelist Jack London declared, "and only then a Socialist."

After the San Francisco earthquake in 1906, four distinguished Japanese seismologists who had come to inspect the damage were stoned by hooligans. Japanese restaurants were boycotted; rotten eggs and fruit were thrown at Japanese laundries, and their drivers were attacked on their rounds. In October the San Francisco Board of Education dug up an old California law that empowered school boards "to exclude all children of filthy or vicious habits, or children suffering from contagious diseases, and also to establish separate schools for Indian children, and for the children of Mongolian and Chinese descent." It required all Japanese and Korean children, as "Mongolians," to attend a separate Oriental school from then on.

Agitation grew on the West Coast for the same prohibition of Japanese immigration as had been in effect against the Chinese since 1882, and early in 1907, President Theodore Roosevelt, with authorization by Congress, debarred any further Japanese arrivals from Hawaii, Mexico, and Canada. The next year the United States and Japanese governments entered into a "Gentlemen's Agreement," under which the Japanese undertook to issue no more passports to skilled or unskilled laborers for travel to the continental United States, though passports could be given to "laborers who have already been in America and to the parents, wives, and children of laborers already resident there." Almost all of the early immigrants had been men, and the latter provision of the Gentlemen's Agreement led to a flood of immigrating Japanese wives—"picture brides," joined to the immigrants in arranged marriages by faraway proxy, which were legal under Japanese law. To the horror of whites, these wives then had a spate of children, who were yellow-skinned citizens.

The Hearst papers, meanwhile, had begun warning of the dangers of a Japanese military invasion. Congressman Richmond Pearson Hobson, a naval hero of the Spanish-American war, writing in late 1907 under the headline JAPAN MAY SEIZE THE PACIFIC SLOPE, had somehow worked it out that an army of the yellow races, led by Japan, of exactly 1,207,700 men could capture the whole Pacific Coast. Two years later, Homer Lea, a hunchback who had become a general in the Chinese army and an adviser to Sun Yat-sen, predicted in *The Valor of Ignorance* the capture of the Philippine Islands by the Japanese, and then their invasion of California, Oregon, and Washington, and finally the total demoralization and disintegration of the Republic, which would "again into the palm of re-established monarchy pay the toll of its vanity and its scorn."

The skill and industry of the Japanese as farmers, alarming to white landowners, led to the passage in California in 1913 of Alien Land Laws, which banned further purchases of land by Japanese aliens and limited their leases on farmland to three years. After the First World War, these Land Laws were made even more strict. "Picture brides" were raising up a generation of Japanese Americans, and organizations such as the American Legion and the California State Grange began to argue that the Gentlemen's Agreement should be replaced by a total exclusion of Japanese. In 1924, the federal immigration law was amended expressly to cut off all further Japanese

POTATO FIELD

"A Mistake of Terrifically Horrible Proportions"

immigration and naturalization. (These rights were not restored until 1952.)

Naked racism had given energy to all these restrictive moves. During the school segregation campaign, one Grove Johnson had written, "I am responsible to the fathers and mothers of Sacramento County, who have their little daughters sitting side by side with matured Japs, with their base minds, their lascivious thoughts." Arguing for the Land Laws, one Ralph Newman said, "Near my home is an eight-acre tract of as fine land as there is in California. On that tract lives a Japanese. With that Japanese lives a white woman. In that woman's arms is a baby. What is that baby? It isn't a Japanese. It isn't white. It is a germ of the mightiest problem that ever faced this state; a problem that will make the black problem of the South look white." "Would you like your daughter to marry a Japanese?" asked *Grizzly Bear,* the magazine of a group calling itself The Native Sons of the Golden West. To the Native Sons, California was "the White Man's Paradise." Their Grand President, William P. Canbu, wrote during the exclusion campaign that "California was given by God to a white people, and with God's strength we want to keep it as He gave it to us."

The news from the Pacific after the first shock of Pearl Harbor grew worse and worse, and nerves in the Presidio tightened. On December 13, the Japanese captured Guam; on December 24 and 25 they took Wake Island and Hong Kong. On December 27, Manila fell, and United States forces retreated to the Bataan Peninsula.

It now began to appear that General DeWitt did not after all have a clear mind of his own. Attorney General Biddle would later write that DeWitt "was apt to waver under popular pressure, a characteristic arising from his tendency to reflect the views of the last man to whom he talked." He started sending Washington rattled and mixed signals.

On December 19, he urged the War Department "that action be initiated at the earliest practicable date to collect all alien subjects fourteen years of age and over, of enemy nations and remove them" to inland places, where they should be kept "under restraint after removal." This recommendation covered only aliens—Germans and Italians as well as Japanese.

Toward the end of the month, DeWitt began talking by phone— outside the normal chain of command, without telling his superiors— with an officer he knew in Washington, a man of his own age, Maj. Gen. Allen W. Gullion. Gullion was Provost Marshal General, the army's top law enforcement officer. Since the fall of France in June 1940, he had been concerning himself with the question of how the military could acquire legal control over civilians in wartime—in case there should be a domestic fifth column—and DeWitt, evidently stung by the ridicule of his alarms by civilian agencies such as the FBI and the FCC, was much attracted by Gullion's views.

DeWitt's own intelligence chief, Lt. Col. John R. Weckerling, was against mass resettlement and internment, and in a call to Gullion the day after Christmas, DeWitt, while he complained that the FBI was not being firm enough against the Japanese, said he doubted the "common sense" of trying to intern 117,000 Japanese in his war zone. Gullion, however, had a different view. He told DeWitt, "I've reached the point where I think I'm going to ask the Secretary [of War, Stimson,] to tell the President the Attorney General is not functioning." Within days, Gullion had the chief of his Aliens Division, Maj. Karl R. Bendetsen, draft a memorandum proposing that the President "place in the hands of the Secretary of War the right to take over aliens when he thought it was necessary," and at the end of the month Gullion sent Bendetsen to San Francisco, with the obvious idea that support for this proposal by "the man on the ground" might help push it through. From that time on, DeWitt, with all of his clout as commander of the western war zone, was putty in the hands of Gullion and Bendetsen.

Karl Bendetsen, then thirty-four years old, was not an army regular. He had earned undergraduate and law degrees at Stanford, the latter in 1939, and, having joined the War Department's judge advocate department in 1940, just out of law school, he would rocket from captain to colonel in two short years. As head of Gullion's Aliens Division, this youngster was soon the army's key man on all Japanese alien and Japanese American affairs. Indeed, he would be able to claim with pride after the war that he had been given the Distinguished Service Medal because he—not General DeWitt or anyone else—had "conceived method, formulated details, and directed evacuation of 120,000 persons of Japanese ancestry from military areas."

In one of their turn-of-the-year conferences, Bendetsen outlined to DeWitt plans for surveillance and control of West Coast Nisei of

sorts that Gullion and Bendetsen knew Attorney General Biddle would never approve; if the Justice Department wouldn't do the job, Bendetsen told DeWitt, then it would be up to the army—really, to the two of them—to do it. According to notes taken at the session, DeWitt went along with Bendetsen, saying that he had "little confidence that the enemy aliens are law-abiding or loyal in any sense of the word. Some of them, yes; many, no. Particularly the Japanese. I have no confidence in their loyalty whatsoever."

Suffering from what Chief of Staff George Marshall called "localitis," and determined not to fall into a disgrace like that of his contemporary, Lt. Gen. Walter C. Short, who had been stripped of his Hawaii command after Pearl Harbor, DeWitt asked for reinforcements for the Western Defense Command. When some arrived, he blew up—too many of them were black. He protested to Washington, "You're filling too many colored troops up on the West Coast. . . . There will be a great deal of public reaction out here due to the Jap situation. They feel they've got enough black-skinned people around them as it is. Filipinos and Japanese . . . I'd rather have a white regiment." A few days later, Lt. Gen. Lesley J. McNair, deputy commander of the Army Ground Forces, told Stilwell, "DeWitt is going crazy and requires ten refusals before he realizes it is 'No.' "

All this time, contrary winds from civilians were blowing General DeWitt's weather vane this way and that. Clamor grew, from organizations like the Native Sons and the American Legion, for the incarceration of all Nisei. The Portland, Oregon, post of the Legion advocated "the removal from the Pacific Coast areas of all Japanese,

Choir, with Director Louie Frizzell

both alien and native-born, to points at least 300 miles inland," resolving "that this is no time for namby-pamby pussyfooting, fear of hurting the feelings of our enemies; that it is not the time for consideration of minute constitutional rights of those enemies but that it is time for vigorous, whole-hearted, and concerted action." California's liberal governor, Culbert C. Olson, on the other hand, had taken the position that Japanese Americans should continue in wartime to enjoy their by no means minute constitutional rights. Congressman Leland Ford of Los Angeles argued for their removal with a most peculiar logic. On January 16 he wrote Stimson a formal recommendation

> that all Japanese, whether citizens or not, be placed in inland concentration camps. As justification for this, I submit that if an American-born Japanese, who is a citizen, is really patriotic and wishes to make his contribution to the safety and welfare of this country, right here is his opportunity to do so, namely, that by permitting himself to be placed in a concentration camp, he would be making his sacrifice. . . . Millions of other native-born citizens are willing to lay down their lives, which is a far greater sacrifice, of course, than being placed in a concentration camp.

There were in fact lots of patriotic Nisei; many of them were fiercely and showily patriotic precisely because so many "real Americans" doubted their fidelity. Some had joined together in the Japanese-American Citizens League, which did all it could to flaunt its members' loyalty. Their idealistic creed, adopted before Pearl Harbor, said, "Although some individuals may discriminate against me, I shall never become bitter or lose faith, for I know that such persons are not representative of the majority of American people." Nisei in many cities and towns helped with civil defense. In the San Joaquin Valley, for example, they signed up as air-raid wardens and did guard duty against sabotage at the Parlier water supply. Furthermore, many young Nisei volunteered for the army. (In Italy and France, beginning two years later, the Japanese-American 442nd Combat Team turned out to be one of the most decorated units in the entire United States Army—with seven Presidential Distinguished Unit Citations, one Congressional Medal of Honor, forty-seven Distinguished Service Crosses, 350 Silver Stars, and 810 Bronze Stars. It suffered 9,486 dead and wounded. In one Distinguished Unit Citation, Lt. Gen. Mark Clark, commander of the Fifth Army, would write, "You are always thinking of your country before yourselves. You have never complained through your long periods in the line. You have written a brilliant chapter in the history of the fighting men in America. You are always ready to close with the enemy, and you have always defeated him. The 34th Division is proud of you, the Fifth Army is proud of you, and the whole United States is proud of you." President Truman, attaching a Presidential Unit Banner to their regimental colors, would say they had fought "not only the enemy, but prejudice.")

DeWitt's anxieties, however, flowered more and more, and they soon bore fruit. On January 21 he recommended to Secretary Stimson the establishment of 135 "prohibited zones" in the coastal states—mostly small circles of about a thousand feet in diameter or rectangles of a few city blocks, from which all enemy aliens would be removed

—as well as a handful of larger "restricted zones," where they would be kept under close surveillance. Many of the "prohibited zones" were along stretches of coastline where DeWitt feared Japanese landings; others were around docks, airports, power plants, pumping stations, dams, and military installations—though strangely none was around any of the big aircraft factories in San Diego, Los Angeles, and Seattle.

On January 25, Stimson recommended to Biddle that DeWitt's zones be established. In his covering letter, it was clear that Stimson had swallowed whole DeWitt's reports of danger. "As late as yesterday, January 24," Stimson wrote,

> he stated over the telephone that shore-to-ship and ship-to-shore radio communications, undoubtedly coordinated by intelligent enemy control, were continually operating. A few days ago it was reported by military observers on the Pacific coast that not a single ship had sailed from our Pacific ports without being subsequently attacked. General DeWitt's apprehensions have been confirmed by recent visits of military observers [i.e., Karl Bendetsen] from the War Department to the Pacific coast.

Since this request touched only enemy aliens, and meant moving them in most cases for very short distances, Biddle acceded to Stimson's urging and began setting up the prohibited areas. He gave Tom C. Clark, who was then chief of the Anti-Trust Division of the Justice Department on the West Coast—and who would later be a justice of the United States Supreme Court—the task of supervising the removal of aliens from the zones.

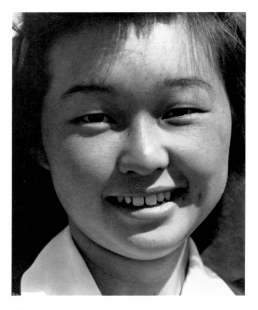

Yuri Yamazaki, High School Student

Clockwise from top left: MASAO
NAKAZAWA, CHEMISTRY TEACHER;
YUMIKO SEDOHARA; HIDEMI TAKENAKA;
MAY ICHIDE, SUNDAY SCHOOL TEACHER;
BERT K. NAMURA.

By this time the intelligence units of the two military services were at odds over the question of how dangerous the ethnic Japanese along the coast really were. On January 26, Lt. Comdr. K. D. Ringle of the Office of Naval Intelligence, Eleventh District, in Los Angeles, submitted a ten-page memorandum to the Chief of Naval Operations, in which he concluded

> that the entire "Japanese Problem" has been magnified out of its true proportion, largely because of the physical characteristics of the people; that it is no more serious than the problems of German, Italian, and Communistic portions of the United States population, and, finally, that it should be handled on the basis of the individual, regardless of citizenship, and not on racial basis.

Ringle's report found its way to both Biddle and the War Department, and it doubtless helped to harden the Attorney General's determination not to have anything to do with a massive violation of the constitutional rights of Japanese Americans.

At the beginning of February, voices raised on the West Coast against Japanese Americans became more and more shrill. The *Los Angeles Times* took up the cry that Japanese citizens were just as much enemies as Japanese aliens: "A viper is nonetheless a viper wherever the egg is hatched—so a Japanese-American, born of Japanese parents —grows up to be a Japanese, not an American."

Next it became clear that Governor Olson was moving off the high ground on which he had earlier taken his stand. In a radio address, he said that the loyalty of Germans and Italians was easier to check than that of Japanese, and he added—evidently having had this from General DeWitt—that "it is known that there are Japanese residents of California who have sought to aid the Japanese enemy by way of communicating information, or have shown indications of preparation for fifth-column activities." He hinted that there might have to be large-scale removals.

Earl Warren, who would, years later, as Chief Justice of the Supreme Court, be excoriated by American conservatives for the ultra-liberal bias of his court's decisions, was then Attorney General of California. He incidentally also had his eye on Governor Olson's job and indeed would win it away from him in the next election. On the day of the *Times*'s "viper" editorial, he convened a meeting of 150 California sheriffs and county district attorneys. A federal government observer reported that Warren opened the meeting with a warning against hysteria, but went on to talk about Japanese Americans "in such a fashion as to encourage hysterical thinking." The observer wrote that the Los Angeles district attorney, Isidore Dockweiler, asserted—all too aptly foreshadowing the later attacks on Warren—

> that the United States Supreme Court had been packed with leftist and other extreme advocates of civil liberty and that it was time for the people of California to disregard the law, if necessary, to secure their protection. Mr. Dockweiler finally worked himself into such a state of hysteria that he was called to order by Mr. Warren. The meeting loudly applauded the statement that the people of California had no

trust in the ability and willingness of the Federal Government to proceed against enemy aliens. One high official was heard to state that he favored shooting on sight all Japanese residents of the state.

Three days later, a nationally syndicated newspaper columnist wrote: "Mr. Biddle is the attorney general—but he could run for office in California and not even win the post of third assistant dog catcher. Maybe feeling is wrong. All I know is that Californians have the feeling that he is the one in charge of the Japanese menace, and that he is handling it with all the severity of Lord Fauntleroy."

Biddle had in fact been the only responsible official who had so far kept his head. He wanted to issue a press release jointly with the army, designed to calm public fears on the West Coast about sabotage and espionage, and on February 4, he, Assistant Attorney General James Rowe, J. Edgar Hoover of the FBI, Stimson, Assistant Secretary of War John J. McCloy, Gullion, and Bendetsen met to discuss it. Gullion later described this encounter:

> [The Justice officials] said there is too much hysteria about this thing; said these Western Congressmen are just nuts about it and the people getting hysterical and there is no evidence whatsoever of any reason for disturbing citizens, and the Department of Justice—Rowe started it and Biddle finished it—the Department of Justice will have nothing whatsoever to do with any interference with citizens, whether they are Japanese or not. They made me a little sore,

and I said, well listen, Mr. Biddle, do you mean to tell me that if the army, the men on the ground, determine it is a military necessity to move citizens, Jap citizens, that you won't help me? He didn't give a direct answer, he said the Department of Justice would be through if we interfered with citizens and writ of habeas corpus, etc.

When DeWitt, on February 9, asked for the establishment of much larger prohibited zones in Washington and Oregon, Biddle refused to go along. "Your recommendation of prohibited areas for Oregon and Washington," he wrote Stimson on February 9, "include[s] the cities of Portland, Seattle, and Tacoma, and therefore contemplate[s] a mass evacuation of many thousands. . . . No reasons were given for this mass evacuation. . . . The Department of Justice is not equipped to carry out any mass evacuation." And if there was any question of evacuating citizens, the Attorney General wanted no part of it—yet in washing his hands of this eventuality, he now conceded that the Army might justify doing this "as a military necessity. . . . Such action, therefore, should in my opinion, be taken by the War Department and not by the Department of Justice."

Two days later Stimson went over Biddle's head to Roosevelt. Unable to fit an appointment into a busy day, the President talked with Stimson on the phone. The Secretary told Roosevelt that the Justice Department was dragging its feet and asked if he would authorize the army to move American citizens of Japanese ancestry as well as aliens away from sensitive areas; and, further, whether he would favor evacuating more than a hundred thousand from the entire West

LINE CREW AT WORK

Coast or would prefer limiting the removals to small numbers around critical zones, "even though that would be more complicated and tension-producing than total evacuation."

Right after Stimson hung up, McCloy jubilantly called Bendetsen in San Francisco to say that the President had declined to make a specific decision about numbers himself but had decided to cut out the Justice Department and had given the army *"carte blanche* to do what we want to do." Roosevelt's only urging was to "be as reasonable as you can."

The very next day—so promptly as to suggest that there had been some orchestration—the most influential newspaper pundit in the country, Walter Lippmann, in a piece titled "The Fifth Column on the Coast," lay out the basis for advocating the removal of citizens as well as aliens. "The Pacific Coast," he wrote,

> is in imminent danger of a combined attack from within and without. . . . It is a fact that the Japanese navy has been reconnoitering the coast more or less continuously. . . . There is an assumption [in the Justice Department] that a citizen may not be interfered with unless he has committed an overt act. . . . The Pacific Coast is officially a combat zone. Some part of it may at any moment be a battlefield. And nobody ought to be on a battlefield who has no good reason for being there. There is plenty of room elsewhere for him to exercise his rights.

A few days later the right-wing columnist Westbrook Pegler passed this message on to his far larger readership. "Do you get what

[Lippmann] says? . . . The Japanese in California should be under armed guard to the last man and woman right now and to hell with habeas corpus until the danger is over."

The day after the Lippmann article, the entire Pacific Coast congressional delegation signed and delivered to Roosevelt a resolution urging "the immediate evacuation of all persons of Japanese lineage and all others, alien and citizen alike, whose presence shall be deemed dangerous or inimical to the defense of the United States from . . . the entire strategic areas of the states of California, Oregon, and Washington, and the Territory of Alaska."

And the next day after that, freed by Roosevelt's green light to the army, doubtless encouraged by Lippmann and by the vociferousness of the West Coast press and West Coast congressmen, General DeWitt finally submitted to Stimson his recommendation for "Evacuation of Japanese and Other Subversive Persons" from the Pacific slope, to be carried out by his command. The Attorney General had written that the army would have to show "military necessity" to justify such a radical action, and DeWitt's astonishing effort to do this needs to be quoted at length:

> The area lying to the west of Cascade and Sierra Nevada Mountains in Washington, Oregon, and California, is highly critical not only because the lines of communication and supply to the Pacific theater pass through it, but also because of the vital industrial production therein, particularly air-

craft. In the war in which we are now engaged racial affinities are not severed by migration. The Japanese race is an enemy race and while many second and third generation Japanese born on United States soil, possessed of United States citizenship, have become "Americanized," the racial strains are undiluted. To conclude otherwise is to expect that children born of white parents on Japanese soil sever all racial affinity and become loyal Japanese subjects, ready to fight and, if necessary, to die for Japan in a war against the nation of their parents. That Japan is allied with Germany and Italy in this struggle is no ground for assuming that any Japanese, barred from assimilation by convention as he is, though born and raised in the United States, will not turn against this nation, when the final test of loyalty comes. It, therefore, follows that along the vital Pacific Coast over 112,000 potential enemies, of Japanese extraction, are at large today. There are indications that these are organized and ready for concerted action at a favorable opportunity. The very fact that no sabotage has taken place to date is a disturbing and confirming indication that such action will be taken.

Here was logic worthy of Orwell's *Animal Farm:* Proof that all ethnic Japanese were "ready for concerted action" lay in their not having taken it yet.

On February 17, Biddle, in a letter to the President, made a last-ditch protest against the idea of mass evacuation. Citing the swelling propaganda for the removal of the Japanese on the ground that inva-

sion and widespread sabotage were expected any day, he wrote, "My last advice from the War Department is that there is no evidence of imminent attack and from the F.B.I. that there is no evidence of planned sabotage." He argued that removing all the Japanese would play havoc with coastal agriculture, and that it would tie up transportation and cause "complete confusion and lowering of morale." He was furious at Walter Lippmann's irresponsibility. "It is extremely dangerous," he wrote, "for columnists, acting as 'Armchair Strategists and Junior G-Men,' to suggest that an attack on the West Coast and planned sabotage is imminent when the military authorities and the F.B.I. had indicated that this is not the fact. It seems close to shouting FIRE! in the theater. . . . "

The protest came too late. By this time the Attorney General—whose voice had been absolutely alone in reminding those in power of central values in the Bill of Rights that should not be recklessly abandoned even in wartime—was not only ignored; he was brutally vilified. Congressman Ford of Los Angeles told later of a call he made to Biddle:

> I called the Attorney General's office and told them to stop fucking around. I gave them twenty-four hours' notice that unless they would issue a mass evacuation notice I would drag the whole matter out on the floor of the House and of the Senate and give the bastards everything we could with both barrels. I told them they had given us the runaround long enough . . . and that if they would not take immediate action, we would clean the god-damned office out in one

sweep. I cussed at the Attorney General and his staff himself just like I'm cussing to you now and he knew damn well I meant business.

By this time, though, Biddle's views had already become irrelevant. On the day he wrote and transmitted this final protest to Roosevelt, Stimson convened a meeting with War Department aides to plan a presidential order enabling a mass evacuation under army supervision. Gullion was sent off to draft it.

That evening McCloy, Gullion, and Bendetsen went to Biddle's house, and Gullion read his draft aloud to the Attorney General. The order was to be sweeping and open-ended. Basing the President's right as Commander-in-Chief to issue it on a war powers act that dated back to the First World War, it authorized

> the Secretary of War, and the Military Commanders whom he may from time to time designate, whenever he or any designated Commander deems such action necessary or desirable, to prescribe military areas in such places and of such extent as he or the appropriate Military Commander may determine, from which any or all persons may be excluded, and with respect to which, the right of any person to enter, remain in, or leave shall be subject to whatever restriction the Secretary of War or the appropriate Military Commander may impose in his discretion.

This was shrewdly drawn in such a way as to cover German and Italian as well as Japanese "persons," whether aliens or citizens—or, for that matter, any "persons" at all—and was not limited to the West

Coast. The army was authorized to provide transportation, food, shelter, and whatever else might be needed to carry out the order. And the jurisdiction over prohibited and restricted zones previously given to the Attorney General was stripped from him and turned over to the army.

Biddle had to face facts. He had been dealt out of the game. The next day he knuckled under and helped polish the order.

And on the day after that, February 19, 1942, Franklin D. Roosevelt set his signature to Executive Order 9066, "Authorizing the Secretary of War to Prescribe Military Areas."

Mr. and Mrs. Dennis Shimizu

On February 20, Secretary Stimson formally appointed General DeWitt "the Military Commander to carry out the duties and responsibilities" under Executive Order 9066. Up to this time there had not been agreement, either in Washington or "on the ground," as to how many and what kinds of people should be evacuated. Some were still thinking in terms of small restricted areas, from which some 60,000 mainly Japanese should be cleared out; others wanted to cleanse the whole area of something like 110,000 Japanese; while still others, among them the future Supreme Court Justice Tom Clark, wanted to purge the area of all German, Italian, and Japanese enemy aliens, perhaps as many as 266,000 people. It was now up to the War Department to set the guidelines.

In his letter of appointment, Stimson specified that DeWitt should not bother to remove persons of Italian descent. There was widespread

"A Mistake of Terrifically Horrible Proportions"

affection for Italian Americans. The Mayor of San Francisco was one, and the baseball stars Joe and Dom DiMaggio, whose parents were aliens, were among the most popular idols in the country. "I don't care so much about the Italians," Biddle later quoted Roosevelt as having said in his cavalier way. "They are a lot of opera singers."

Stimson—and his subordinates, in subsequent memos to DeWitt—took a slightly harder line on German aliens, though they never authorized evacuating German Americans. Instructions to DeWitt were that German aliens who were "bonafide refugees" should be given "special consideration." In any case, the FBI had long since taken into custody German aliens who had been marked as potentially subversive.

As to ethnic Japanese, the message was clear. Classes 1 and 2 of those who were to be moved out were "Japanese Aliens" and "American Citizens of Japanese Lineage." A sharp racist line had been drawn.

DeWitt's instructions from Stimson and his aides did not specify the most important questions of all: when the evacuations should begin, from exactly what areas the removals should be carried out, where those evicted should be held, and exactly who should take charge of their removal and incarceration.

These questions were resolved in the following days during a period of greater hysteria than ever on the West Coast. Congress had set up a select committee to investigate the need for what it euphemistically called "National Defense Migration," and, testifying in San

Francisco on February 21, Earl Warren echoed DeWitt's amazing "proof" of trouble to come. Unfortunately many people, he said,

> are of the opinion that because we have had no sabotage and no fifth column activities in this State . . . that none have been planned for us. But I take the view that this is the most ominous sign in our whole situation. It convinces me more than perhaps any other factor that the sabotage we are to get, the fifth column activities we are to get, are timed just like Pearl Harbor was timed and just like the invasion of France, and of Denmark, and of Norway, and all of those other countries.

Two evenings later, almost as if by design to make irrational fears like these seem sane and plausible, a Japanese submarine, the I-17, having recently returned to the coastal waters, fired thirteen five-and-a-half-inch shells at some oil storage tanks on an otherwise empty hillside north of Santa Barbara. No hits were scored. But was this a prelude to an invasion?

The next night the army detected (nonexistent) enemy airplanes over Los Angeles, and at three o'clock in the morning an antiaircraft battery opened fire. Other gun crews, hearing the explosions, began firing, and within a couple of hours 1,400 three-inch shells had gone off above the city. Their fragments rained down, causing a fair amount of damage to automobiles. It took quite a while before this happening could be given the joking title it came finally to bear: "The Battle of Los Angeles." At the time, it reinforced the public's panic.

On February 27, the Cabinet in Washington met to discuss how

Mr. and Mrs. Dennis Shimizu

the evacuation should be carried out. Bendetsen had been arguing that the army should not bear the burden of administering the removals because, as he said in a phone call to the State Department, the army's job was "to kill Japanese, not to save Japanese." And indeed, the Cabinet did decide that day—in order to make sure that not too many combat troops would be involved in the process—that the "resettlement" should be handled by a new civilian agency, which would eventually be called the War Relocation Authority. Milton S. Eisenhower, an official of the Department of Agriculture, brother to the popular general who would one day be elected President, was put in charge of it. The arrangement would be this: The army would be responsible for rounding up the evacuees and moving them to temporary collection centers, and then the civilian WRA would move, settle, and hold them for the duration of the war in permanent camps.

On March 2, General DeWitt issued his first proclamation under Executive Order 9102, which had spelled this out. In it he stretched the arm of his authority far beyond the small prohibited and restricted zones he had earlier set up, for he now established as Military Area No. 1—the field of hottest imaginary danger—the entire western halves of Washington, Oregon, and California, and the southern half of Arizona. Presumably somewhat cooler was Military Area No. 2, comprising all the remainder of the four states.

General DeWitt did not yet, however, issue any orders for actual removals, because in Washington Gullion had realized that there was no law on the books that made a civilian's disobedience of a military command a crime, so there was no way for DeWitt to force anyone to move. Gullion's office therefore went to work drawing up a statute—something absolutely new in American legal history—that would invent such a crime. General DeWitt urged that imprisonment be mandatory, and that the crime be classified as a felony because, he argued, "you have greater liberty to enforce a felony than you have to enforce a misdemeanor, *viz*. You can shoot a man to prevent the commission of a felony."

On March 9, Stimson submitted to Congress the proposed legislation, which would subject any civilian who flouted a military order in a military area to a year in jail and a fine of five thousand dollars. Only one person in either house rose in debate to challenge this law: the arch-conservative Senator Robert A. Taft, who would be known in later years as "Mr. Republican." This bill, he said, was "the 'sloppiest' criminal law I have ever read or seen anywhere." But when it came to a vote, not even he opposed it. Not a single member of either house voted against the bill, which was signed into law by Roosevelt on March 21.

Taft's scruple points up a fascinating aspect of this entire tale of error: The few scraps of opposition to the drift of hysteria that led to the incarceration of American citizens had tended to come from borderline reactionaries like J. Edgar Hoover and Robert Taft. Even Francis Biddle, though he took a much freer view than others, was a patrician of the old style, whose wish to hold to the Constitution was essentially conservative. On the other hand, many of those who had been swept along by the wave of malign fever were, or would be seen in time to be, leading liberals: for example, Earl Warren, Culbert Olson, and even, in his grand offhandedness, Franklin Roosevelt. Impeccably liberal attorneys such as Benjamin Cohen, Oscar Cox, and Joseph Rauh had drafted rationalizations for evacuating Japanese Americans, given "military necessity." And as we shall see, liberal Supreme Court justices such as William O. Douglas and Hugo L. Black would endorse the removals.

There had in fact been three theories to justify the evacuations. The first, held by DeWitt, was purely racist—that loyalty was automatically determined by ethnicity. The second, held by those on middle ground, was also essentially racist: that "inscrutable Orientals" came from a culture so foreign to the Greco-Roman, Judeo-Christian culture that it was impossible to make out whom among them to trust. As Bendetsen would put it, "You couldn't determine loyalty, and therefore you had to take the wheat with the chaff." The third view, taken by decent conservative bureaucrats wedded in their posts to army bias, men like Stimson and McCloy, was that loyalty was a matter of individual choice, but in a time of danger of sabotage and attack like that in 1942, there simply wasn't time to do the necessary winnowing. The terrible flaw in this last view was that the danger they perceived had been imagined by DeWitt.

While legal enforcement was being legislated, DeWitt, McCloy, Bendetsen, and others at first encouraged "voluntary" resettlement— a notion that has to be put in quotation marks because it was obvious to those who "voluntarily" moved that they were being pushed out.

Bendetsen argued that the army shouldn't advertise that it would house and feed evacuees, since there would then be a rush of freeloaders. But it was soon clear that voluntary evacuation would not work. For one thing, people inland were inhospitable. "I do not desire," Governor E. P. Carville of Nevada wrote DeWitt, "that Nevada be made a dumping ground for enemy aliens to be going anywhere they might see fit to travel." Besides, very few were inclined to leave their land and sell their goods to take up an unknown new life in some strange place. Of 107,500 ethnic Japanese in Military Area No. 1, only 4,889 moved of their own accord. On March 27, DeWitt issued Public Proclamation No. 4, which *forbade* ethnic Japanese in Military Area No. 1 changing their residence unless ordered or permitted to do so by the army.

In the meantime, during the period of the so-called voluntary removals, the army had been searching for appropriate assembly centers in which it would hold the evacuees until the WRA was ready to take them off to permanent camps. With the posting of Civilian Exclusion Orders beginning on March 31, 1942, as we have seen, the cruel capture of the ethnic Japanese—this horrendous black smudge on the American record of freedom—was set in motion.

As to the fate of the evacuees in what must have seemed to them their endless captivity, we have the solemn testimony of the photographs and text of this book. The detainess could not be held forever. The winding down of this awful mistake was almost as tortuous and shameful as its making.

By early 1943, Stimson, Marshall, McCloy, and others in the War Department and army had clearly seen that "military necessity" could no longer, by the wildest imagining, justify keeping loyal American citizens of Japanese ancestry—or even loyal aliens, of which there were evidently many—away from the West Coast in "pens." Milton Eisenhower of the War Relocation Authority had never been comfortable with the resettlement program. Earlier, in the fall of 1942, McCloy had begun to urge a loyalty review that would make possible the formation of a Nisei combat team. General Emmons, the commander in Hawaii, applauded; Nisei, he thought, would make "grand soldiers"—as indeed they did. In January 1943, Stimson announced the formation of the combat team with a ringing declaration: "It is the inherent right of every citizen, regardless of ancestry, to bear arms in the Nation's battle."

Dewitt was horrified. He realized that loyalty reviews in the camps would undermine the entire exclusion policy. On the very day on which McCloy received word that the combat team would be formed, DeWitt called Gullion and said, "There isn't such a thing as a loyal Japanese, and it's just impossible to determine their loyalty by investigation—it just can't be done." He then called McCloy and said that undertaking loyalty reviews would be "a sign of weakness and an admission of an original mistake. Otherwise—we wouldn't have evacuated these people at all if we could determine their loyalty."

Bendetsen, who had been a lead actor in the campaign to purge the coast of "Japs," was now beginning to waver. To one of McCloy's aides he remarked, "Of course [the fact that loyalty is hard to deter-

Kenji Sano

Top, left to right: RYOHE NOJIMA, FARMER; CORPORAL JIMMIE SHOHARA; MITSUO MATSURO.
Bottom, left to right: KAY FUKUDA, U.S. NAVAL CADET NURSE; MORI NAKASHIMA.

mine] is probably true of white people, isn't it? You know that old proverb about 'not being able to look into the heart of another'? And 'not even daring to look into your own.'" And to another aide: "Maybe our ideas on the Oriental have been all cock-eyed. . . . Maybe he isn't inscrutable." But Bendetsen agreed with DeWitt that for the War Department to unravel the exclusion policy would be to "confess an original mistake of terrifically horrible proportions. . . . I would find it very hard to justify the expenditure of eighty million dollars to build Relocation Centers, merely for the purpose of releasing them again."

As rumors of a possible easing of the exclusion policy reached the West Coast, there came a new surge of racist clamor. The California American Legion passed a resolution suggesting that it wasn't enough to keep ethnic Japanese in concentration camps—they should be deported. Various groups alleged that the evacuees were being "pampered" and "coddled." In April, DeWitt testified before the House Naval Affairs Committee, decrying "the development of a false sentiment on the part of certain individuals and some organizations to get the Japanese back on the West Coast. I don't want any of them here. They are a dangerous element." Under the heading DEWITT IS RIGHT, the *San Francisco Chronicle,* dismissing "the ethical factors, the constitutional factors, the question of the Bill of Rights," warned that the return of the evacuees would mean riots. A *Los Angeles Times* editorial argued that to end the restraints on the Japanese, with their "record for conscienceless treachery unsurpassed in history," would be, as the headline of the editorial put it, STUPID AND DANGEROUS.

In June, Chief Justice Harlan Fiske Stone of the Supreme Court, writing a majority opinion against Gordon Kiyoshi Hirabayashi, a student at the University of Washington who had refused at the inception of the resettlement to report for evacuation, seemed to take the position that racism was not necessarily barred by the Constitution. "The adoption by the Government," he wrote, "in the crisis of war and of threatened invasion, of measures for the public safety, based upon the recognition of facts and circumstances which indicate that a group of one national extraction may menace that safety more than others, is not wholly beyond the limits of the Constitution." Justice Douglas, concurring, showed that the court, like the War Department before it, had been taken in by DeWitt's alarms after Pearl Harbor. "We cannot," he wrote, "sit in judgment of the military requirements of that hour."

Armed with this support, DeWitt redoubled his arguments against any easing of the exclusion. The breaking point between the general and the War Department finally came when he began to fight hard against letting soldiers take leaves and furloughs in the excluded area. McCloy insisted, and he got Stimson and Marshall to support him. A Jap might be a Jap in DeWitt's eyes, but a GI was a GI in McCloy's. National sentiment, away from the West Coast, had turned against DeWitt. The *Washington Post* wrote: "The general should be told that American democracy and the Constitution of the United States are too vital to be ignored and flouted by a military zealot." Finally, in the autumn of 1943, the War Department had had enough of DeWitt's obsessive fears and complaints. He was relieved of his western Defense Command.

DeWitt's departure did not, however, mark the end of all this. Politics intervened. Late in 1943, with DeWitt gone, Attorney General Biddle spoke up once more. Arguing to Roosevelt that "the present practice of keeping loyal American citizens in concentration camps for longer than is necessary is dangerous and repugnant to the principles of our Government," he urged that the WRA be placed under the humane charge of the Interior Department. This was done. In the spring of 1944, the War Department itself finally urged the President to bring the exclusion to an end, and Secretary of the Interior Harold Ickes wrote Roosevelt urging him to act at once: "The continued retention of these innocent people in the relocation centers would be a blot upon the history of this country."

Others, however, urged caution. Under Secretary of State Edward Stettinius, Jr., for instance, reminded the President in a memorandum: "The question appears to be largely a political one, the reaction in California, on which I am sure you will probably wish to reach your own decision." Roosevelt's decision was to waffle. He proposed something manifestly impracticable—a gradual dispersion of the evacuees to other parts of the country besides the West Coast. The unmentionable political fact underlying this delaying tactic was that Roosevelt would be running for a fourth term as President in November. The evacuees would have to wait.

Roosevelt was reelected. Not long afterward the Supreme Court, in two cases, *Korematsu* v. *the United States* and *Ex parte Endo,* again failed to find the exclusion policy unconstitutional. In the Korematsu case, the majority swallowed whole the "military necessity" that DeWitt had invented in his *Final Report.* In the Endo case, however, while Justice Douglas's opinion did nothing to challenge the constitutionality of the evacuations, it did rule that an admittedly loyal American citizen could not be held in a concentration camp against her will.

At the first cabinet meeting after the election, a decision was reached to end the exclusion. Those evacuees who passed loyalty reviews could, at last, go home.

Relocation Departure

They went home to a bitter freedom. It took a year to empty all the camps. Given train fare and twenty-five dollars in cash, the evacuees returned to the coast and, according to an Interior Department report, "piled into temporary shelters, hotels, converted Army barracks, and public housing." Many learned that their stored goods had been stolen or sold; their land had been seized for unpaid taxes; strangers had taken possession of their former homes. They faced vicious racist hostility. An attempt was made to blow up an evacuee's fruit-packing shed; shots were fired into homes that evacuees had managed to reclaim. Jobs were plentiful on the coast at the time, but not for the returning detainees, who faced notices: NO JAPS WANTED. Housing was hard to find. Whole families moved into single rooms. Many women had to take live-in domestic work for the sake of beds to sleep in. One man, who had a brother still overseas with the 442nd Regimental Combat Team, would testify that his mother "finally had enough money for a down payment on a house. We purchased the house in 1946 and tried to move in, only to find two Caucasian men sitting on the front steps with a court injunction prohibiting us from moving in because of a restrictive covenant. If we moved in, we would be subject to $1,000 fine and/or one year in the county jail."

One ordeal had ended; another had begun. All of the returning Nisei faced the task of rebuilding ruined lives.

POSTSCRIPT

Years passed. The nation underwent new agonies: the Vietnam War, student unrest, the assassinations of two Kennedys and of Martin Luther King, Jr., race riots in the cities, plagues of drugs and greed, a sexual revolution, and the shame of Watergate. These stresses brought deep and irreversible sea changes in the country's mores and values. Two incidental signs that some of these changes were for the better: Federal district courts ruled that in the *Hirabayashi* and *Korematsu* cases, American citizens had been improperly interned, and two Japanese Americans, Daniel Inouye and Spark Matsunaga, both much-decorated veterans of the Nisei 442nd Regimental Combat Team, achieved the honor of election to the United States Senate. The country was apparently ready at last to take another look at the wartime treatment of Japanese citizens and aliens. It turned out, however, to be an agonizingly long, slow look.

In 1980, Congress established a Commission on Wartime Relocation and Internment of Civilians with a mandate to "review the facts and circumstances surrounding Executive Order 9066," and to make recommendations for "appropriate remedies." In the last half of the next year, the Commission took testimony from more than 750 witnesses, and a year after that, in December 1982, it finally submitted its report. Entitled *Personal Justice Denied,* this document unsparingly peeled back, for all to see, the complex layers of national guilt.

In 1984, in the Ninety-eighth Congress, the first of a series of bills was introduced to make amends to those whose lives had been so cruelly hurt. Hearings were held, but the congressional term ran out before action was taken, and the bill died. The next year, another bill was introduced and died. In 1987, Senator Matsunaga and seventy-three cosponsors introduced a third bill in the Senate, and a similar bill was launched in the House of Representatives.

This third round of bills proposed that every surviving internee would receive $20,000, free of taxes, and—more important—an apology from the government of the United States. As there had been no distinction made between citizens and aliens in the commission of the injustice, so there was none in the amends, for the apologies and recompense would go not only to those who had been citizens at the time of the evacuations, but also to those who were then aliens. The money, amounting altogether to $1.2 billion, would be paid out in stages, over four years, to the estimated sixty thousand surviving internees—to the very old first, and then to less and less aged survivors. Heirs of internees who died before the bills became law would receive nothing.

The twin bills did not ride through with ease. Whereas the Justice Department under Attorney General Francis Biddle had fought almost alone against internment, now, under Attorney General Edwin Meese, the department objected to the apology for it, and to the amount of money in the proposed recompense. When the House voted on its bill in September 1987, *more than a third* of its members voted nay. In

"A Mistake of Terrifically Horrible Proportions"

the Senate, Senator Alan Simpson of Wyoming said, "An apology is way overdue, but coupling it with money takes away some of the sincerity." Senator Jesse Helms of North Carolina argued, in the face of settled facts to the contrary, that the internment was justified because intelligence reports to President Roosevelt had indicated that some Japanese Americans were enemy agents, and he proposed an amendment (which was defeated) to "provide that no funds shall be appropriated under this title until the government of Japan has fairly compensated the families of men and women who were killed as a result of the . . . bombing of Pearl Harbor." When the Senate bill was passed in April 1988—nearly eight years after Congress had first been moved to do something about this blot on the nation's conscience—a smaller number of Senators (sixty-seven) voted in favor of it than had sponsored it in the first place the year before.

On August 10, 1988, President Ronald Reagan finally signed the nation's belated act of contrition. With that rounding out of the story the time had come to recall the initial, crucial question: Could anything like all this happen ever again in the United States of America?

A PORTRAIT OF MANZANAR

By John Armor and Peter Wright

THE NISEI

Who were the people brought to Manzanar at gunpoint?

They shared only one common characteristic: "a Japanese ancestor in any degree."

Two-thirds were first-generation American citizens. They lived in American cities, attended American schools, and thought of themselves as Americans. That belief was sorely tested when, by order of President Roosevelt—an order carried out by General John L. DeWitt, West Coast Commander, and his subordinates—they were removed from their homes, schools, and businesses, and brought to Manzanar and nine other camps like it. The first-generation Japanese Americans were called, in Japanese, *Nisei*.

A few were second-generation Americans, called *Sansei*. Neither they nor their parents had ever known any other life than their life in the United States.

Almost a third of the prisoners were Japanese citizens, resident aliens by definition of the U.S. immigration law. They were called *Issei*. All of this group had lived in the United States at least eighteen years, since American borders were closed to Japanese immigrants in 1924. All had been specifically barred from applying for American citizenship. The right to become an American citizen was not allowed

CHOIR GROUP

to the Japanese until 1952, when quotas were introduced.

Because the Issei would have become American citizens, given the opportunity, the Issei and the Sansei are sometimes described generically as Nisei.

The Nisei were diligent and able people. More than one-third of the adults were farmers. Almost a quarter were merchants, shopkeepers, and others in retail trades. Many were fishermen. A few were professionals. But no matter what their trades or professions, when they were moved, most of them lost everything: farms, shops, boats—everything. Professionals, for the most part, lost the opportunity to practice their skills.

Those who had owned their homes—and many did—lost them, along with most of their furniture and possessions, when they were incarcerated. The government had offered written assurances that their possessions would be stored and protected when the Nisei were "relocated." In fact, no such storage areas existed at the time. A half-hearted effort to establish them was made a year later by the Federal Farm Mortgage System, but it was too little, too late. In almost every case, the Nisei's possessions were lost in the frenzied, six-day periods between the time each evacuation order was posted and the Nisei were taken away to the camps.

Not all the camps were located in American deserts, but all were deliberately isolated from towns or cities of any size as a matter of policy. The government euphemistically labeled Manzanar and the others "War Relocation Camps," but, simply put, they were concen-

MORI NAKASHIMA, IN CHICKEN FARM

tration camps—a fact even the army initially acknowledged in documents as it was building these facilities—since only a certain segment of the general population was affected, detained by force in areas where they could be watched and controlled.

The preparation of Manzanar to receive prisoners began in June 1941, six months before Pearl Harbor. It began as a "military" installation known as Camp Owens. It was planned as a tent city to hold up to ten thousand people. It had an airstrip next to its front gate. After initial preparation, it contained only a contingent of about twenty military police.

A letter to General DeWitt from Colonel Karl R. Bendetsen of May 20, 1942, refers to "an Emergency Plan for evacuation if developments require." The letter said, "It was impossible, of course, at this time for the Army to reveal the fact that it was prepared to effect a complete evacuation, practically overnight, in the event of an emergency. Plans were made to move the 113,000 Japanese into already-established Army containments in a mass movement, which could have been undertaken immediately."

Camp Owens, at Manzanar, was one of those "Army containments" prepared before Pearl Harbor. It may have been the central one, since Colonel Bendetsen's letter refers to a "Reception Center" as the only one of eighteen containments other than race tracks, fairgrounds, and other readily available, large-scale facilities.

Advance preparation for internment of the Nisei is also indicated by the fact that on November 26, 1941, President Roosevelt asked Henry Field, an anthropologist, to prepare a list of all Nisei in the

United States and the communities where they lived, using the 1930 and 1940 censuses. While the Census Bureau denies its confidentiality was breached, within a week Field delivered that list to the President.

The possibility of taking "Japanese" hostages (ignoring the fact that most of the Nisei were American citizens) as either a control device or bargaining chip with Japan arose in early 1941. We were then negotiating with the Japanese about "spheres of influence" in the Pacific.

Describing Manzanar and the others as "concentration camps" conjures horrible images of the ovens of Dachau under the Nazis, or the Soviet Gulag in Siberia. As bad as they were, the American concentration camps never approached the horrifying conditions of the camps in Europe. There were no gas chambers or medical "experiments" at Manzanar or the other American camps. There were no attempts to work prisoners to death.

In fact, the food and the medical care at Manzanar were better than adequate, in large measure because the Nisei were given the opportunity to provide for themselves.

There was one other difference separating the American concentration camps from the European camps. In most instances, families were kept together. The Nisei prized the institution of the family. It may be this difference, more than all others, that allowed them to survive and prosper under very difficult circumstances.

The numbers alone tell an important part of the internment story. Only 1,875 Nisei from Hawaii, each individually identified as a pos-

CATHOLIC CHURCH

sible threat to the security of the United States, were interned. The rest of the 120,000 prisoners were from the mainland. Manzanar was the first of ten camps to open. The following list identifies all the camps, their first and last days of operation, and the maximum number of prisoners held at any time in each—and offers a stark picture of the Nisei's fate:

Gila River, Arizona	Aug. '42–Nov. '45	13,400
Granada, Colorado	Sept. '42–Oct. '45	7,600
Heart Mountain, Wyoming	Sept. '42–Nov. '45	11,100
Jerome, Arkansas	Nov. '42–June '44	8,600
Manzanar, California	June '41–Nov. '45	10,200
Minidoka, California	Sept. '42–Oct. '45	9,990
Poston, Arizona	June '42–Nov. '45	18,000
Rohwer, Arkansas	Oct. '42–Nov. '45	8,500
Topaz, Utah	Oct. '42–Oct. '45	8,300
Tule Lake, California *	June '42–Mar. '46	18,800
Total †		114,490

* There were two camps at Tule Lake. The second was a high-security prison for the 3,500 Japanese Americans believed to pose individual threats to the United States' war effort. None was ever charged with or convicted of spying or sabotage. Still, this small group was not released until long after the war was over.
† This figure does not reflect the fact some prisoners were released before others were interned. The total number of "evacuees" was more than 120,000.

Toyo Miyatake Family

Only What They Could Carry

In typical bureaucratic fashion, the War Relocation Authority published its pamphlet, *Questions and Answers for Evacuees, after* the Nisei had been rounded up and taken to the camps. Solid information about what was happening was scarce, and what was provided was often misleading and euphemistic, as this definition in the relocation booklet testifies:

"Relocation Center—A pioneer community, with basic housing and protective services provided by the Federal Government, for occupancy by evacuees for the duration of the war."

There were 108 Evacuation Orders issued. With military precision, the areas of Nisei population were divided into groups of about one thousand, each under the jurisdiction of a Civilian Control Office. Private arrangements were made among the various government agencies involved, with no public announcements. Then, on six days' notice, the Orders were posted in the target areas.

Civilian Exclusion Order No. 1 applied to Bainbridge Island in Puget Sound, outside Seattle, Washington. Bainbridge was the first target because the island was largely populated by Nisei, and because all ships going in and out of Seattle Naval facilities passed close by it.

On March 21, 1942, Order No. 1 was posted. On March 26, 276

LOADING BUS TO LEAVE MANZANAR

residents of the island, most of them American citizens, were transported directly to Manzanar. The Caucasian resort areas on the island were not affected by the Order.

Manzanar was the first camp ready to receive "residents," so the people from Washington State were sent there. There had been one prior evacuation. At the insistence of the navy, on February 11, 1941, the President signed an executive order giving it jurisdiction over Terminal Island in Los Angeles harbor. For decades it had been a fishing village of Nisei. On February 25 the navy ordered all residents to leave within forty-eight hours.

Many of the men had already been arrested for the "crime" of owning or working on fishing boats. They were put in prisons or stockades. Under this new Order, their wives and children were transported to Manzanar.

Three of the next nine Evacuation Orders were posted in Los Angeles in ten days after March 21. Almost all of the people affected by these Orders were sent to Manzanar. Seventy-six percent of the population of Manzanar came from the city of Los Angeles. Ninety-two percent came from Los Angeles County, including then-rural areas such as San Bernardino.

On August 11, 1942, the final Order, No. 108, was posted in Tulare County, California. Under all Orders a total of 92,193 people were taken by the military into "Assembly Centers." The Assembly Centers were constructed primarily at fairgrounds and race tracks.

As they were transferred, the Nisei were permitted to take on the buses and trains that transported them to the prisons only what they

PEOPLE LEAVING BUDDHIST CHURCH, WINTER

could carry in their hands. Men, women, and children arrived with suitcases or bundles tied with string, containing only a small fraction of their clothing and personal possessions.

In fact, most had already lost almost everything. As the Evacuation Orders were posted in each district, the Nisei were usually given six days to wind up their affairs and report to Civil Defense centers for transport. During that time, the Caucasian "neighbors" of the Nisei gathered like vultures to purchase homes, businesses, furniture, and personal possessions for whatever the market would bear—in most cases, at about ten cents on the dollar.

While most Nisei didn't see the *Questions and Answers* booklet until after they got to the camps, the booklet contained the following reassurances about the storage and transport of personal possessions left behind.

> *Question 2:* Before I leave for an Assembly Center should I sell or store my household goods?
> *Answer:* Keep in mind that you will be going to a war-duration Relocation Center . . . and that many of your household goods will be needed at your new home . . . So do not needlessly dispose of or sacrifice things you may need . . . Your household goods may be stored for you free of charge while you are at the . . . Center, provided you box and crate these goods suitably.

Those who had left homes and possessions with Caucasian friends learned too late that arson, theft, and vandalism eventually claimed many of their possessions, as "anti-Jap" groups, using tactics

*The State legislature has just passed
the "Lowery Act," which provides for
the seizure of idle farm machinery and
has received the approval signature of
California Governor Earl Warren. . . .*

*[The act] refers not just to farm
machinery and equipment of evacuees
but to everybody's . . . [It is] too early to
know [the] effects. Also, of course, [the]
constitutionality of the act has not been
determined.*

*[As a matter of fact, the bill only
affected the imprisoned Nisei farmers.
The Caucasian farmers could all
demonstrate that their machinery and
equipment were "in use."]*
May 26, 1943 Manzanar Free Press

similar to those of the Ku Klux Klan, swung into action. Most Nisei were already left with nothing but what they carried into the camps by the time they passed the signs that said, WELCOME TO MANZANAR, or WELCOME TO TULE LAKE, or WELCOME TO ROHWER.

The Nisei lost property valued at between $810 million and $2 billion dollars (in current dollars) due to the forced evacuation, according to estimates in *Personal Justice Denied*, the final report of the Commission on Wartime Relocation and Internment of Citizens. The Commission was established in 1981 to investigate and report on the effects of the wartime internments. Its recommendations, published in June 1983, placed the value of total losses of property and income in 1942–45 as high as $6.2 billion (in current dollars). Yet as high as these figures are, they do not attempt to account for the personal damages done to individuals imprisoned without charge, trial, or conviction.

Behind the statistics lie thousands of individual stories.

Mrs. Tetsu Saito, born in 1900, was a widow living in a low-income neighborhood in Los Angeles when she testified in 1981 before the Commission on Wartime Internment. Before the war, her family had owned the Ruth Hotel in Los Angeles, a thirty-two-room building valued then at six thousand dollars. By 1942 they had paid off the mortgage.

When they were ordered to evacuate to Manzanar, a Caucasian offered them three hundred dollars for their hotel. Having little choice, they accepted it. They also had sixty-four crates of possessions and six trucks, all of which were lost or stolen while they were confined. After Manzanar closed, the family moved to a trailer park in Lomita.

Henry Murakami was a fisherman living on Terminal Island in Los Angeles. Like many Nisei fisherman, he was arrested and jailed, not merely interned. He lost three purse-seine nets valued at $22,000. His pregnant wife and four children had only forty-eight hours to prepare to go to Manzanar. "She couldn't carry anything except clothing . . . We had a three-bedroom house with a kitchen. My wife had to abandon everything . . . the furniture and all of our other furnishings, including a 1940 Plymouth . . . no one ever knew what happened to my property."

Yoshio Ekimoto was a Nisei, born in 1914. His family owned a forty-acre farm in northern Los Angeles County. His parents had bought this farm in 1912, the year before California passed a law making it illegal for Japanese aliens to own land in the state.

Ekimoto was interned at Poston, Arizona, in May 1942. He was one of the few who was able to keep accurate records of his losses.

When he returned home in 1945, his farm had been completely mortgaged. He was forced to sell it to pay the mortgage. He had listed all the personal property he lost while he was interned, down to cameras, boxes of shotgun shells, and the attorney's fees he incurred (five dollars) in trying to avoid what inevitably happened to him and his family.

The sending of over two thousand absentee ballots to the Japanese evacuee citizens in assembly and relocation centers has brought divergent views, mostly critical, in the metropolitan newspapers of Los Angeles. The majority of the people interviewed by one reactionary Hearst newspaper have said the Japanese should not be given the privilege of voting since the Japanese are wards of the federal government.

In these critical times when the nation is exerting tremendous effort to bring decency and justice for all people, regardless of race, color or creed, the arguments presented by [these] people . . . seem to show that they are playing into the hands of the Nazi propagandists."

AUGUST 26, 1942 MANZANAR FREE PRESS

His total losses came to $23,824 in 1942 dollars, which represents nothing of the additional personal harm suffered by him and his family, including his wife's miscarriage as a result of the internment. He was paid a total of only $692 in compensation under the 1948 Evacuation Claims Act.

TAR PAPER
AND BOARDS

The barracks at Manzanar were constructed of quarter-inch boards over a wooden frame, the outsides of which were covered with tar paper nailed to the roof and walls with batten boards. Heat was provided by oil-burning furnaces. This was the cheapest, quickest way to provide living quarters slightly better than tents. At Manzanar, the cost of this construction was $3,507,018, or $376 per inmate.

According to army regulations, this type of housing was suitable only for combat-trained soldiers, and then only on a temporary basis. The army called this "theater of operations" housing. But at Manzanar and the other camps, these barracks were used as long-term housing for men, women, and children—who stayed in them for up to three and a half years.

In many ways, *Questions and Answers for Evacuees* glossed over, in soothing bureaucratic language, the ramifications of the Nisei's evacuation and the circumstances they would encounter in the camps. The booklet was fairly accurate, however, when it warned the Nisei to be prepared for temperatures varying from "freezing in winter to 115 degrees in . . . the summer." Manzanar provided both of those extremes, plus wind that whipped the snow across the desert in the winter, and dust in the spring, summer, and fall. Among all the camps,

MANZANAR STREET SCENE

the extremes of temperatures endured by the Nisei ranged from 130 degrees in Poston, Arizona, to minus thirty degrees in Heart Mountain, Wyoming.

The main camp at Manzanar consisted of 560 acres, on which were constructed nine wards of four blocks each. Each block contained sixteen barracks, or one-story buildings, twenty by one hundred feet. Of the sixteen buildings, fourteen were residential, one of double size was the mess hall, and the last was a meeting/recreation hall. The barracks were divided into "apartments" of various sizes. According to *Questions and Answers for Evacuees,* a family of four could be expected to be assigned a twenty-by-twenty-five-foot "apartment."

In fact, an average of eight people were assigned to each of these "apartments," with the number rising as high as eleven, depending on the size of the families involved. Smaller families were grouped together in single apartments. Furnishings consisted of iron cots, bags to be filled with straw, and three army blankets for each prisoner.

Each block had communal kitchen and dining hall buildings, and communal bathhouses. Except for the Caucasian staff, who lived in separate quarters, there were no private facilities.

Most "residents" were confined to the main camp, an area surrounded by guard towers and barbed wire. Outside the main camp, but inside the second perimeter of barbed wire, lay another 5,700 acres, of which more than 1,500 acres were farmed before Manzanar closed. Only the Nisei who were assigned to farm work were allowed in this area.

Mr. and Mrs. Henry J. Tsurutani and Baby Bruce

Masako Tabuchi . . . thought that she would set the world right about the conditions prevalent in the assembly centers. Every word she uttered was the truth, but stating the truth is not always the best way to gain a point. . . . She said, in part, ". . . That we have not complained is not an indication that we have not suffered. . . . We are accorded the fullest freedom as long as we keep 10 feet within the bounds of the barbed wire fences. . . ."

This "ungrateful and petulant note" incurred the wrath of many readers of the San Francisco Chronicle. *Those who were inclined to feel sorry for the "poor mistreated Japanese" stiffened. . . .*

It is a fundamental tenet of applied psychology that people do not like to be reminded of mistakes and shortcomings. Though many Americans feel sympathy for the tragedy that befell the Japanese in America our reminding them of it will not erase the condition, nor will it insure their continued sympathy.

OCTOBER 22, 1943 MANZANAR FREE PRESS

PEOPLE LEAVING BUDDHIST CHURCH

The main camp was surrounded by guard towers equipped with searchlights and machine guns. Several Nisei were shot and killed at Manzanar, though not during attempted escapes; they died when guards fired into unarmed public demonstrations prompted by the actions of the camp's unpopular first director.

Manzanar was constructed as a complete city. Its hospital had 150 beds, the normal size for an American city of ten thousand people. Despite the primitive living conditions and the climate, and the large number of women, children, and elderly prisoners at Manzanar, hospital use never exceeded 50 percent of capacity. In health as in other matters, the Nisei at Manzanar proved to be exceptionally self-reliant and strong.

農場

Benji Iguchi, on Tractor in Field

Of Farms and Farmers

Almost half of the Nisei were farmers by training. Their skills were based on a tradition of thousands of years of tilling poor land and making it productive. They had proved their skill in America over decades, buying or leasing the poorest and cheapest land in California, Oregon, and Washington, and growing fine crops on it.

Aided by the emergency sale bargains obtained during the evacuations, and by a 1913 California law prohibiting Japanese aliens from owning land, neighboring farmers were quickly able to close in on Nisei farms and take them over. The productivity of the farms immediately dropped everywhere except in Hawaii, where almost all the Nisei were allowed to remain on their farms.

At Manzanar, the Nisei found themselves in a desert, a wholly different agricultural environment. Water had to be allocated from the Los Angeles Aqueduct watershed for their farms and facilities.

Yet within a month, fields were planted, first with guayule, a plant from which rubber could be extracted. Rubber was essential to the war effort, and supplies from South America were becoming unreliable.

Next, food crops were planted—sweet corn, cucumbers, melons, radishes, turnips, tomatoes, and watermelons. To support those crops,

MANZANAR

9 1

the Nisei designed and constructed an irrigation system to divert nearby Symmons Creek into the Manzanar water system and increase its irrigation capacity.

By August, just four months after the camp was populated, three hundred acres were under cultivation. Initially, work efforts were limited because there was only one plow. Farmers worked in three shifts. Just a year later, 1,500 acres were under cultivation at Manzanar. The Nisei also revived some of the orchards from which Manzanar took its name. By the end of that August, up to six hundred lugs of apples and five thousand boxes of pears were ready to be picked.

By September 1942, the storehouses were filled with the harvested crops. Manzanar became not only self-sufficient in feeding itself, but also shipped its excess crops to other camps to feed the prisoners there.

There were a few indigenous farms still left in the valley when Manzanar was created. None of them—over a span of decades—had ever equaled the yields that the Nisei coaxed from the dry and stony fields of Manzanar.

By the summer of 1943, the Nisei had obtained cattle and swine, plus chickens, ducks, and other farm animals. Manzanar thus became self-sufficient in meat and poultry as well as crops. It provided meat and poultry to the other camps, and sold excess crops, meat, and poultry on open markets. Proceeds of sales went to the camp administration.

Agricultural production reached a total of $800,000 at four camps, including Manzanar, in 1942. By 1943, it had risen to a staggering $2,750,000. Manzanar was a leader among camps in the pro-

duction of livestock and poultry, contributing strongly to an estimated $2,000,000 production value in fiscal 1944. (By the summer of 1944, the population of the camps was beginning to decline.)

Providing food for the nation—civilians and military personnel—was an important part of the war effort of the United States. By this criterion alone, the Nisei at Manzanar did as much for the United States during World War II as any other city of comparable size in the country and more than some, despite real handicaps of climate and circumstances.

Ironically, although the Nisei were very productive in the camps, their internment still significantly impeded the war effort in food production. The government spent $4,114,036.31 in 1942 alone to subsidize "substitute operators" for the former farms of the Nisei. These were Caucasian farmers who took over the land, buildings, equipment, and crop-growing operations, but could not maintain the productivity levels of the Nisei. And at the same time, of course, the army spent another $3,054,925.46 just to imprison the Nisei.

Manzanar was not unique in its impressive farm yields. Records of the other nine camps show similar agricultural achievements, though most were constructed too late to farm effectively in the summer of 1942. Some overcame even rougher climatic conditions than those at Manzanar.

The Nisei also served the nation on farms outside the camps. Caucasian farmers faced massive crop losses in the summer of 1942, owing to the lack of migrant workers. Their representatives asked for help from the White House in May. By mid-October, ten thousand

Benji Leuchi with Squash

RICHARD KOBAYASHI,
FARMER WITH CABBAGES

*Building 33-15, a temporary warehouse
to store banana squash harvested from
the local farm, collapsed Sunday
morning at 10:33 A.M. The squash was
stored four feet high with an estimated
[weight] of 190,000 pounds.*

*The entire 100 foot structure . . .
collapsed eastward two feet, with the
southeast corner forced open 3 feet by
the weight. All of the outer beams were
believed to be broken.*
OCTOBER 27, 1943 MANZANAR FREE PRESS

Nisei were put on leave from the camps, working as seasonal agricultural laborers. Demand for these workers far exceeded supply. Once the harvest seasons were over, of course, they were returned to the camps.

These workers faced discrimination and harassment on the job, and their living conditions were far worse than those back in the camps. Still, thousands volunteered, and are credited with saving the sugar beet crops of several western states.

店舗

MASAKO SUZUKI, IN CO-OP STORE

THE MANZANAR COOPERATIVE

Like any city, Manzanar required all the ordinary supplies for daily living: everything from cloth, needles, and thread to shoes, heavy coats, toothbrushes, and razors. But at Manzanar, when the "residents" arrived, there were no stores making such items available. Eventually, a government-operated camp store opened, but the supplies and products it offered were minimal at best.

Many of the Nisei had been successful merchants in their hometowns in California, Oregon, and Washington. Now their stores and stock in trade were gone; most of their money was gone, too—but their skills remained.

Within weeks the former merchants had planned the Manzanar Cooperative, which also did a thriving mail-order business. Every adult was asked to contribute $5 to the operating capital of the co-op. By the end of 1943, almost 100 percent of the adult population had joined. Some had that much money in hand. Others saved it from their wages of up to $12 a month for the women, or up to $19 a month for the men. Between May and November 30, 1942, the co-op had already done a business of $342,979.88.

The Manzanar Consumer Cooperative was set up to own and operate any and all kinds of necessary businesses, none of which were planned or operated by the government. Such a large operation required careful cultivation, and an election was held on June 30, 1942, in which all residents over the age of sixteen voted for delegates to the congress of the Manzanar Cooperative Enterprises. The congress, in turn, appointed a board of directors to run the canteen, department store, and other community enterprises. All businesses paid rent to the government for the use of buildings and space.

The original board of directors for the co-op were self-appointed volunteers, but in August 1942, the co-op held its first elections for members of the board. Thereafter, it was run by an elected board, and profits were distributed at the end of the year among the membership.

The co-op was incorporated as a profit-making venture under the laws of California. The profits were designated for the members of the co-op, or to be paid to such community-service and public-assistance purposes as the board should direct.

Within weeks of the opening of Manzanar, and before any legal structure had been set up, the co-op had opened makeshift stores in a barracks, and was selling basic supplies. Within two months the co-op had grown into a small department store, offering all the basic necessities that could be found on the main streets of any small American town.

Also within two months, the co-op began advertising its wares in quarter-page ads taken in the *Manzanar Free Press*. It bought wholesale and sold retail, offering sturdy goods at reasonable prices. It usually bought supplies for cash, from those who would not extend credit, but in some cases the co-op obtained its wares on credit from

Plans have been made by the Consumers Enterprises and Ansel Adams whereby photographs of Manzanar taken by the noted photographer will be sold to those who desire them. . . .

Co-op states that orders will be taken by numbers only. The prices are as follows: contact prints, 15 cents, 8 × 10 prints, mounted, $2, 11 × 14 prints, mounted, $2.50, unmounted, $2.15. . . .
FEBRUARY 2, 1944 MANZANAR FREE PRESS

suppliers who knew and respected the business abilities of the Nisei managers.

In all, the co-op consisted of a general merchandise store, a dry-goods store, a newspaper and magazine stand, a mail-order desk, a shoe-repair shop, a barber shop, a beauty shop, and a laundry and cleaning depot. After two months, it employed 185 Nisei.

In its first complete year, 1943, the co-op achieved total sales of $812,351.72; employment expanded to 222 people full time; and the venture turned a profit of $79,180.89 for its members. Its assets at the end of 1943 were $119,054.63, with liabilities of $38,111.44.

By the summer of 1944, when the war ended and Manzanar was closed, the co-op had grown to a $1-million-per-year business, supplying all the commercial needs of the isolated "city" in the desert. Not only was it able to supply Manzanar's internees with whatever goods they needed, but it did not do so as a monopoly, for it competed from early on with larger, outside merchandisers.

The first of these to offer goods to the "residents" of Manzanar was Sears, Roebuck. Quarter-page ads from Sears in Los Angeles appeared in the *Manzanar Free Press* in June 1942, in the same issue that ran the first co-op ads. Other outside businesses followed.

But the co-op was the only supplier to offer credit to the Nisei; the others required payment in advance. As a result, the co-op served not only as a department/hardware/dry-goods store, but became a successful bank for the Nisei as well. On those operations, too, it made a modest but steady profit.

Again we go to bat for the beauty parlors. With all equipment installed, even to the mirrors, operators selected, the only thing that holds up the grand opening is the adamant objection of the Block 15 residents where the beauty parlor is to be located. . . .

As time goes on there will be more and more projects that must be temporarily housed in the laundry rooms. Must the Community Enterprises [the co-op] and the administration continually bicker and argue with block residents about the establishment of a project that will benefit all the people?
OCTOBER 12, 1942 MANZANAR FREE PRESS

The success of the co-op was based on the skills of the Nisei who had been successful merchants and businessmen even before they were imprisoned at Manzanar. But there was one skilled group among the Nisei that was largely unable to practice during the years of imprisonment. For some of them, the damage they incurred followed them for the balance of their lives.

Warehouse: M. Ogi, Manager; S. Sugimoto, Co-op Manager; and Bunkichi Hayashi

Professionals Without Professions

再

業

Dr. Kiyoshi Sonoda was a graduate of the University of Southern California, and a practicing dentist in Los Angeles. When the war began he volunteered for the Dental Corps, but was turned down on the grounds it would be "bad for morale." One brother had volunteered for the army in 1940 and was in the coastal artillery in San Francisco. He was transferred to Kansas. Another brother was a pharmacist, serving as a narcotics agent for the Treasury Department. He was transferred to Baltimore.

Dr. Sonoda and his entire family voluntarily moved to Fresno in 1942, where Nisei were then permitted to live. Later the boundaries of "exclusion" were expanded, and the entire family was forced into the Gila River Camp in Arizona. But there were too many dentists at that camp, or, rather, there were initially too few supplies and too little equipment for all to do their work.

When another dentist took his place at Gila River, Dr. Sonoda and his family were allowed to leave the camp for Colorado. There, he and another dentist took the State Licensing Board exams. Both were refused the right to practice. They were given no grades; they were simply voted down.

Dr. Sonoda was later turned down for a position in Detroit, on racial grounds. Finally he found another position in Detroit, but only after the War Relocation Authority intervened on his behalf, because USC would not forward a copy of his credentials.

Then, when the war ended, this man who had been turned down by the army as a volunteer dentist, was drafted as one, and returned as a military dentist to California, where he had begun.

Dr. Sonoda's experience was typical of many professionals in all camps. He was restricted in practicing his profession inside the camps, and later suffered from limited professional opportunities on the outside.

The doctors imprisoned at Manzanar were more fortunate. There were three graduates of USC, one from Rush Medical School, and one doctor of public health from Johns Hopkins. They were allowed to practice at the camp, though they were seriously hampered by a lack of adequate equipment and supplies. Despite their training, they were paid only nineteen dollars per month, the same wage as any skilled laborer. The Caucasian doctor who was in charge of Manzanar's medical staff and hospital, on the other hand, was paid his usual fee.

The original operating room, constructed at the end of one of the barracks, perhaps best exemplifies the working conditions for Manzanar's doctors. Cracks in the wall were open to the wind and dust. They were routinely stuffed with torn sheets. Near the end of July 1942, the new 150-bed hospital was completed. The operating theaters and wards were primitive but adequate; the hospital also included a laundry, so bloodstained sheets no longer had to be washed by hand.

MICHAEL YONEMITSU AND HARRY SUMIDA

An Army Inspection Report on November 13, 1942, described the hospital staff at Manzanar as one Caucasian doctor and a Japanese staff of six doctors (one of whom was pregnant), five practical nurses (one of whom was sick in the hospital), five dentists, ten registered nurses, five senior student nurses, two X-ray technicians, one dental technician, and one optometrist. (The team also found that there was insufficient hot water in the orphanage, no dental chair, no proctoscope, and a shortage of ordinary supplies and medicines.)

Still, despite a lack of equipment and supplies, the Nisei staff provided a high volume of services. Between mid-May and July 27, 1942, for example, almost five thousand dental cases had been handled in the original makeshift clinic.

A contemporary history of Manzanar, written by students in 1942, perhaps summed up the situation best by quoting a certain Dr. Goto at the camp, who observed, "So far we have been lucky—only two men in the hospital, and nothing much serious there. . . . We've had a few cuts and sprains and a lot of blisters—after all, you expect that when you try to make sagebrush cutters out of good lawyers and accountants."

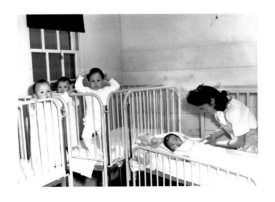

NURSERY, ORPHAN INFANTS

EDUCATION WEEK SIGN

COMMITTED TO EDUCATION

Education was important to the Nisei. They always sought the best possible education for their children in elementary school and high school. Those with the capacities were encouraged to go to college and to graduate schools. And education did not end there; classes in both practical and artistic fields were often organized and run locally for adults of all ages.

A common characteristic of the Nisei in their hometowns, this commitment to education was part of what they brought with them to Manzanar.

The first school event at Manzanar was bittersweet. Bainbridge High School, on Bainbridge Island, in Washington's Puget Sound, sent to Manzanar diplomas for thirteen of their students who had been taken into custody before the school year ended. On June 5, 1942, these high school students became the first of hundreds to graduate behind barbed wire. In a ceremony at Building 3-19, these students received their diplomas from the camp director of Manzanar, Roy Nash, on behalf of Bainbridge High, and heard a special message from their former school principal and the school superintendent of that district. Six students also received Torch Honor Society pins for academic excellence.

Manzanar's first director of education was Dr. Genevieve Carter, who was appointed by the State of California to run the camp's schools. When she arrived in June, Dr. Carter found two thousand students already organized in classes under volunteer instructors. The students brought chairs from their apartments, or used benches made from scrap lumber. They met in "recreation" barracks, which were simply open halls without furnishings.

Their materials and books were limited to several hundred textbooks sent from Los Angeles area schools for the use of students who had been taken from that district's classrooms in March. By July of that first year, classes were formalized under the guidance of three Caucasian teachers, who received salaries competitive within the school district, while the Nisei, for the same work, received only sixteen dollars per month.

Also by July, seven nursery and kindergarten schools were set up, with about fifty children in each. These too suffered the usual shortages of supplies, no classroom partitions, no playgrounds or equipment.

Eventually, two elementary schools, a high school, and an auditorium seating one thousand students were constructed by the "residents," who provided all necessary labor. In time, the schools became fully accredited within the California school system, in every case meeting or exceeding all state standards for education. Children sixteen years of age or under were expected to attend school unless they had work permits and permission from the school to work.

Questions and Answers for Evacuees had promised that "one of

BIOLOGY CLASS, HIGH SCHOOL:
NIYO YOSHIDA, LILLIAN NAKATOSHI,
AND YOSHIKO YAMAZAKI

What Was Manzanar?

In years to come, when the war is over, and peace has returned to the world, people may say to you, "What was Manzanar?" Then I hope you will say that Manzanar was a war time city that sprang up from the sands of the desert of Inyo and returned to desert at the end of the war. It was the largest city between Los Angeles and Reno. It was a city serving a war time purpose where people lived in peace and good will, where there was a school system that taught young citizens the ideals of American citizenship, where schools were of as high a rank as other California schools, and where students dedicated their future lives to the American way of living. [From Director Merritt's message in the Manzanar High School Yearbook for 1943, reprinted in the Free Press.*]*

June 20, 1943 Manzanar Free Press

the first jobs of the War Relocation Work Corps will be to build schools and school equipment at Relocation Centers. Nursery schools, elementary schools, and high schools will be maintained." From the beginning, however, there were too many students and not enough teachers.

Initially, regulations required that all teachers be Caucasian. Of necessity, the regulations were changed to allow the Nisei themselves to serve as teachers, though one strict requirement remained: all classes had to be conducted in English. Japanese could not be spoken in any classroom, for any course, even as a second language or as an aid to students who knew no English.

On March 7, 1943, the first senior class graduated from the Manzanar High School. In a speech, Director Merritt told the eighty-five assembled seniors and their families that he hoped "these young men and women will go out and show the rest of the world the commendable spirit and courage which they have shown as representatives of the majority of the people here."

After the graduation ceremony (in mess hall No. 1), there was a dance with a local band. But despite the party, none of the Nisei could forget that this ceremony took place in a prison.

Approximately 3,500 of the Nisei who were interned were college students from West Coast universities. Robert Sproul, president of the University of California at Berkeley, took the lead in seeking to transfer these students to other universities across the United States. Milton Eisenhower, the first director of the War Relocation Authority (and

Boulder, Colorado—When the Navy Department's Japanese language school, conducted here by the University of Colorado, recently graduated . . . "the largest group of Caucasians ever to learn Japanese," a signal honor was conferred upon that 90 percent of the faculty consisting of niseis.

Capt. Frank H. Roberts, director of all Navy courses on the campus, presented each of these instructors with an engraved certificate "for outstanding faithfulness and diligence despite conditions of racial unrest," thus testifying to the fact that the school's grand achievement could not have been accomplished without these "Americans with Japanese faces."

OCTOBER 2, 1943 MANZANAR FREE PRESS

VOLLEYBALL

later president of Johns Hopkins University), encouraged this effort, as did numerous religious, business, and cultural leaders, through an organization called the National Student Relocation Council.

None of the students who were able to transfer out of the camps received any help with their tuition. They received only enough money to get them to their destinations. Despite the relocation program, many universities refused to accept the Nisei, regardless of grades or clearance from the WRA. Still, by 1944, almost 4,300 students had enrolled in colleges away from the West Coast, a number that included graduates of the camp high schools as well as college students who were removed from the West Coast.

When the camps were closed, most Nisei moved to the Midwest or the East. The children reentering regular elementary, junior high, or high schools couldn't transfer in the normal sense: they did not name their previous school, or provide a transcript; they simply listed the name of the "town" where they had "lived" in those years.

In purely educational terms, the students at Manzanar did well; they kept up with their grade levels, and in many instances surpassed them. Other than the emotional problems that were to be expected from their concentration camp experiences, these students' performances were as exceptional after Manzanar as they were before it.

Even some college-level classes were offered at Manzanar, including business courses. But for the most part, college-age students there either worked or joined the army. Enlistment levels for both young men and young women at Manzanar were higher than in towns of comparable size across the country, and after the war, many Nisei veterans attended college on their GI benefits.

Adult educational programs of various types were also organized at Manzanar. They often combined both practical and artistic elements, such as dressmaking and design, written and spoken English, psychology, weaving, agriculture, photography, journalism, and choir, among many others. Most of these classes were organized as interest demanded, and were offered free of charge.

Apprenticeships in various functional services at Manzanar provided another avenue for education. These were not designed solely as educational programs but were intended as work; still, the Nisei emphasis on learning meant that even helpers were well trained in plumbing, electricity, welding, carpentry, furniture making, teaching, nursing, and many other professions.

The surest way out of Manzanar, other than the army, was through jobs. During the war, skilled workers were in short supply across the country. Except on the West Coast, the Nisei were welcome workers (though they were often paid lower wages than others), provided they had the right skills and were competent in English. A benefit of both the formal and informal educational programs at Manzanar was to provide both the work and language skills that allowed many of the younger "residents" to get out long before the process of closing the camps began.

Sept. 1—10 A.M. Left good ole Manzanar for points east. When you leave the gate, it's like waking up from a dream. The trip to Reno was swell. Who asked for the malt? I had that and also fried chicken, steak, hamburger and hot dog. Come on, now, aren't your mouths watering yet? Got my divorce from Manzanar at Reno. Now I'm free.

At present I'm lying in front of a log fire on a nice rug listening to swell music and writing to you. Freeport is a wee town with old-fashioned houses. . . .

So long, folks. Adios, muchachos, companieros de mia.

Claire Seno
SEPTEMBER 22, 1943 MANZANAR FREE PRESS

SCHOOLCHILDREN

A GENUINE LIFE

Two cultural traditions among the Nisei helped them survive the psychological burdens and physical difficulties of life in the prison camps. The first was the concept of *on*, which denotes the lifelong obligations of every citizen to his government and to his parents.

The second was *giri,* or the obligation to the dignity of one's name. It means, in essence, a deep sense of self-respect. Regardless of circumstances, no matter how difficult or humiliating, it is the obligation of each person to accept those circumstances, and to behave well despite them. As former Senator S. I. Hayakawa put it in testimony to the Senate Committee on Civil Service, in 1984, "One has to do what one has to do, quietly and with dignity."

This sensibility was reflected in the Pleasure Garden that the Nisei constructed in the middle of Manzanar. A few representatives were allowed to go to Yosemite National Park, under armed guard, and to select and bring back the trees, lumber, and stones needed to build a garden around the only running water in the camp, Bairs Creek.

The park was constructed on their own time and included picnic grounds, ball fields, and a stage for both live performances and programs featuring recorded classical music. They also provided on their own a public address system, records, and record players.

POOL IN PLEASURE PARK

A former employee of Paramount Studios, a free-lance Hollywood technical director, and the former proprietor of a Los Angeles amusement hall got together and organized the Community Players. Programs presented by this group included music, singing, and dancing, attracting audiences of up to 1,500 a night.

Apart from its recreational activities, Manzanar had a very effective system of self-government. In open elections the people chose block leaders, each of whom represented about three hundred people. These people were responsible for a wide variety of daily concerns, from dealing with complaints by neighbors about others, to keeping the head count of all "residents" in their blocks.

The initial "election" took place on June 10, 1942, with the blocks making recommendations but camp director Roy Nash making the final selections. The first true election at Manzanar took place on June 20, for blocks 19, 25, 26, 27, and 30. Representatives from these blocks were chosen solely by ballot. Together, the block leaders functioned as an unofficial city council. At Manzanar this system remained in place until the camps were closed.

Here, leaders could be the elders of the community. At all the other camps, such respected elder members were not allowed to take part in camp government if they were not U.S. citizens—and usually they weren't, because they had been barred since 1924 from applying.

The federal courts had no jurisdiction over the camps, and Inyo County and its courts had little interest in taking on cases from Manzanar. So the block leaders' council set up an arbitration system that functioned like a court. Only major crimes, of which there were very

ENTRANCE AT CATHOLIC CHAPEL

First step toward the filling of an obvious gap was the tentative formation of a labor council last Tuesday night. . . . With over seventy departments already operating, involving over 5,000 workers, and with many more industries planned, a vigilant labor council should . . . guarantee the smooth operation of intricate human machinery. . . . We suggest that this council be composed of delegates from every department . . . trusted workers elected by their fellow workers and not Japanese department heads. They will form an impartial body to bring all labor difficulties to the attention of the administration. . . . Out of the experiences of the Idaho workers we must learn our first lesson. . . . We should send experienced men. They should . . . [have] a governing body and a set of rules before they ever leave the center. . . . Fortunately, we are blessed with understanding administrators. But without our help and initiative they cannot do much. Let us make the proposed labor council one of the firmest stones in the foundation of a workable democracy in Manzanar.
July 24, 1942 Manzanar Free Press

few, were referred outside to Independence, the seat of Inyo County.

The Judicial Committee Hearing Board consisted of three Nisei: a block leader, a lawyer, and a social worker. Three others were Caucasian employees chosen by the director. This board recommended actions to be taken officially by the camp director; normally the board's recommendations were followed.

On July 22, 1942, the Hearing Board decided its first case, finding five youths guilty of assaulting a Mr. Kawamura. Director Nash suspended the sentence but reprimanded the boys severely.

One by one, all the institutions and services that would normally exist in a city of ten thousand people were established at Manzanar, including the Bank of America, which opened a branch there in June 1942, and initially conducted business only on Tuesdays.

The first industry created in Manzanar produced camouflage nets for army gun emplacements, beginning in June 1942. A month later, that business employed 516 workers, who produced more than five hundred nets per day. Within six months, employment and production nearly doubled.

This community also observed the kinds of public ceremonies common to small towns, though sometimes with an ironic twist. On July 4, 1942, the residents organized public ceremonies, band concerts, picnics, an "all-star" baseball game, and a beauty contest. Fireworks were planned, too, but were canceled, probably for security reasons. Although the article in the *Manzanar Free Press* does not

BASEBALL GAME

MR. AND MRS. HIRATA AT
YMCA BUILDING

mention them, it is likely that the Girl Scout and Boy Scout units at Manzanar also took part.

The Boy Scouts were active at all the camps. Manzanar, which was recognized as an independent district by the Boy Scouts of America headquarters in New York, organized its fourth troop shortly after the Fourth of July.

Churches of many denominations, and other institutions, such as the Young Men's Christian Association, were established by the Nisei at Manzanar as quickly as the camp director made space available for them.

The Nisei's deeply felt sense of public duty and self-respect, the enlightened administration of Ralph Merritt, Manzanar's second director, and a system of self-government that allowed the natural leaders of the community to remain in leadership roles, all contributed to the development of a humane, coherent life among these people. Still, none of them could forget their situation even for a moment, that they were crowded into tar-paper barracks, that they had no telephones or automobiles, that they were not free to leave, or that at the perimeter of their "town" the military police patrolled with loaded weapons.

THE MANZANAR FREE PRESS

新聞

Manzanar's own newspaper was born on April 11, 1942, when a group of ex-newspapermen vowed to fulfill a vital need for accurate information in the camp. In its first issue, they wrote, "Truth must be the keystone of this community so we have called this the *Manzanar Free Press.*" With the blessing of Manzanar's public relations director, Bob Brown, the premier issue referred to itself as "America's youngest and one of the most unique nespapers." Bob Brown was also head of the Office of Official Reports. This office cleared, and censored, all internal and external documents published in Manzanar for its inmates or the outside world, including the *Free Press*, which could not have existed without its approval.

The first issue of the *Free Press* was four pages long, printed on an erratic mimeo press. Several issues later, it grew to six pages. Having begun as a biweekly, in a month it was published three times per week.

Improvements continued, and three months later, in July, editor Chiye Mori closed volume one and began volume two as a typeset newspaper with an expanded staff. This issue carried ads from Josephs Dry Goods in nearby Lone Pine, California, for mail-order clothes (starting at $1.79 for twill slacks); from the camp canteen, for LaVida

Soda Water and other products, such as cigarettes; for Sears Roebuck in Los Angeles; for the Community Enterprises Department Store (which was part of the Nisei-run cooperative); and for yarns, window shades, witch hazel, Dr. Scholl's foot pads, Colgate tooth powder, and Red Goose shoes. There were also assorted personal ads.

From the beginning, the *Free Press* was entirely self-supporting, at first through subscription sales and then through advertising also. Newspapers were five cents an issue or six dollars for a year's subscription. In addition, one issue was delivered free to each block for those who could not afford to buy it. Classified advertising cost thirty-five cents for twenty-five words—"Tell the story of your product to our thousands of readers in Manzanar and other centers. Write Advertising Manager, *Manzanar Free Press*, for rates."

National and international reporting was provided by clippings gleaned from large and small publications and newspapers across the country.

Roy Takeno was born in Fresno in 1913, and majored in journalism at the University of Southern California. He was working in public relations and for newspapers when he was sent to Manzanar. There he became Information Head for the beet-harvesting effort in October 1942. Later he became Acting Reports Officer in the Office of Official Reports, which made him, in effect, the editor-in-chief of the *Free Press*. His New Year's Day editorial in 1944 (see page 129) was carried on wire services and was favorably received across the nation.

This issue of the *Free Press* was chosen as a representative one,

ROY TAKENO, EDITOR

since it was published after the camp and the newspaper were well established and after the process of allowing some of its inmates to leave had begun. The span of articles shows the breadth of the newspaper's coverage.

MAY 1, 1943:

> Forty-seven persons have gone out this week since Thursday, and fifty-seven last week, Rush Cushion, chief escort, disclosed, adding that an average of fifty residents leave in one week (for resettlement outside the camp). [In the same issue were articles about the demand for stenos and typists in the Civil Service, and the Eastern Defense Command opening some areas of New England for resettlement.]

> Certified by the Federal government as a loyal American, Fred A. Hiraoka, former resident of this center, became Chief Engineer for [a] radio station in Hastings, Nebraska, recently. Fred is a native of Lahaina, Maui, Hawaii, and has been living in the continental United States for the past 11 years. He [holds] a first class radio-telephone operator's license.

> He . . . was evacuated to this center a little over a year ago. He is replacing Chief Engineer Duanne B. Allison who is entering the Army after serving the station for the past two years.

From the editorials, same day:
> The evacuees' moral and spiritual stamina comes to its second significant test in this resettlement issue. They weathered

the first test at the time of evacuation. How successfully we acquit ourselves in the process of resettlement may largely determine what now may seem . . . to be our uncertain postwar destiny in America.

From the advertisements, same day:
IN APPRECIATION As we leave this center, may we take this means to express our appreciation for the kindness extended us during our stay at Manzanar. Mr. and Mrs. Arthur Hiraga and family.

From the advertisements, same day:
YOU DON'T NEED TO WAIT ANY LONGER TO GET OUT [headline on full-page ad by the Utah-Idaho Sugar Company, with this text:] Sugar beets are the best way out for the greatest number of evacuees. When you accept a beet contract, take one with the organization that pioneered the way for evacuee job seekers nearly a year ago; take one with an organization that can give you a wide choice of locations and climates.

This editorial from the *Free Press* was widely reprinted in newspapers across the country and received considerable editorial approval in the outside press. Even after forty-five years, it still seems remarkable that a man who was in prison for his ancestry could write these words about his nation, the United States of America.

ROY TAKENO AND STAFF

January 1, 1944:

Greetings to you for a Victorious New Year, people of America; from your kindred 50,000 citizens inside the barbed wire fences. We send you greetings, we who have been lodged by circumstances of war inside these Relocation Centers in the deserts of the West.

In three months we will have spent two years in these centers. The tragic experiences of evacuation, the business losses of the evacuees, the unwarranted hatreds engendered by some people because of our hereditary kinship with the Asiatic foe—these we write off our ledger. . . .

In seeking to resettle and re-establish ourselves in our respective trades, businesses and professions, we realize the unwisdom of trying to force ourselves upon a people who view us with suspicion. . . . We are prepared to shoulder our share of further sacrifices. We will not shirk. . . . [Some] who have already left are contributing to our embattled nation's war effort in Europe and the South Pacific. . . .

We ask you, the American people, to try us on our own merits, realizing it is one of the characteristics of the country we love to appraise its people by the contribution they can make toward the total welfare of the nation.

This was the end of the line for the *Free Press*. A mimeographed resettlement newsletter continued for several months afterward, but the masthead of the *Free Press* was retired with this issue.

The final issue of the newspaper reported these stories, among others:

Editor Roy Takeno and Group
Reading Paper

The block clearance program closed six blocks and moved remaining residents from four more blocks.

The Children's Village (for parentless children) closed, with the few remaining children moved to Block 2 until they left. The remaining co-op certificates were called in. All community activities closed down.

The *Free Press* said good-bye to the community and recounted the newspaper's history from beginning to end. The final advertisement for Ansel Adams's book, *Born Free and Equal,* appeared. Copies were available at the co-op for one dollar each. The *Free Press* was then down to five staff members.

Some 3,000 Nisei troops were designated by General Francis Oxx to lead the V-J parade in Leghorn, Italy. Manzanar had 1,592 terminal departures, between December 21, 1944, and July 28, 1945, the least number of departures among all centers. The Manzanar co-op advertised its final sale, selling out to the bare walls.

The contrast between the article that appeared about Tulare County and the valedictorian editorial of the *Free Press* could not be sharper. Unfortunately, some of the attitudes reflected in the article, and denied in the editorial, still persist in the United States today.

"WOODLAKE, TULARE COUNTY [CALIFORNIA]—Opposition to return of Japanese evacuees to . . . Tulare County was expressed at a mass meeting in Woodlake, recently. . . . More than 100 persons attended to hear one speaker declare, 'Ethnologically, socially and economically the Japanese are a liability rather than an asset' to the community."

The Last Step

In just three months Manzanar, one-time "home" to more than 10,000 people, will be only a memory—a memory of joy and heartache, happiness and fear, of love and hate. . . .

During these three and a half years we have learned the importance of cooperation, patience, and sympathy in order that others not suffer needlessly. We have made lasting friends among people who face the same problems as we do. They will not be easily forgotten.

But now the time has come when we must find a place for ourselves in a normal community. Our children must know what life is beyond the barbed wire. They have yet to see the bright lights of the city, the traffic signals, streetcars, schools, the corner drugstore, and a million other things that even adults have forgotten. . . .

But wherever we go, we must begin again with a renewed faith to build for ourselves and those of our heritage a place of security in this great nation so that our children will never be forced to experience the loss and hardships that we have known these last few years.

Kiyoko Nomura, Editor, *Manzanar Free Press*

Southwest View: Dust Storm over Manzanar

The Control of Words and Ideas

The army set the terms and conditions for the operation of the internment camps, but the decision first to imprison the entire Nisei population, and then the methods for dealing with them in the camps, were heavily influenced by public opinion and by positions taken by public officials, especially in California.

The army's position on education conducted in Japanese was the same as that reflected in a Report of the Joint Committee on Un-American Activities of the California Legislature, in 1943, which read in part: "It is estimated that there were more than 240 Japanese language schools in California alone. Some 19,000 Japanese boys and girls attended these schools before Pearl Harbor. It is estimated that nearly $400,000 was spent in 1941 for the Japanese educational program directed from Tokyo.

"Many of these schools were found to be under the direction of Shinto priests. They taught the intense nationalism of Japan and the committee is in possession of information and evidence that many of the schools were centers of Japanese propaganda and espionage."

The California legislature failed to note that these schools were conducted after the public school day had ended (as were, and are, Hebrew schools), that all of the children attending them were Ameri-

Roy Takeno (right), Town Hall Meeting

can citizens, or that the parents themselves supported these schools from meager wages and incomes (much like urban parochial schools). Significantly, none of the claimed "evidence of espionage" from the schools was contained in this lengthy Report of the Joint Committee.

In the camps, policy forbade any classes or meetings of any type from being conducted in Japanese. They were conducted in English so that camp administrators could understand all that was said.

Manzanar's first director also cultivated informants among the population as a way to learn of any potentially secret activities. In December 1942, one of these informants was beaten up in his apartment. His attackers wore masks, but he nonetheless identified one of them, who was arrested and jailed outside the camp.

The next day, a crowd gathered at the Administration Building, demanding the release of the man charged. Ralph Merritt, who had replaced Nash as director only a few days before, asked the camp leaders to tell the crowd that the man charged would be returned to Manzanar, but kept in custody. The leaders apparently told the crowd, in Japanese, that the prisoner would be returned and released.

That night, when the prisoner was not released, the crowd gathered again. No one in the crowd was armed, nor was there any attempt at escape, though such an effort that night might have been successful: an army inspection team had reported only four weeks before that four guard towers lacked electricity for the spotlights, none had telephone connections, and the fence had not been completed. Most of this work had not been done when the incident occurred.

The crowd advanced on the Administration Building. Soldiers

fired into it, killing three young men and wounding about ten others. This event was later referred to as the "Manzanar Uprising."

Merritt abandoned the policies of his predecessor. He chose to govern the camp by working through and with the Nisei leadership openly instead, and there were no more such shootings at Manzanar. Merritt did continue, however, to require that all public meetings of any type be conducted in English.

The Office of Official Reports was the headquarters of the *Manzanar Free Press*. Although the day-to-day operation of the newspaper was in their hands, Merritt retained the power to censor or remove from the paper any articles he chose, though in fact he interfered very little with the publication of the paper. As a result, at Manzanar the paper printed not only local stories but national and international ones, too, ranging from coverage of Los Angeles City Council meetings (three-quarters of the readers of the *Free Press* were from L.A.) to war news from both Europe and the Pacific.

Merritt also allowed the *Free Press*, beginning in its second year, to publish a Japanese-language edition for those detainees who could not read English, which was contrary to the policy at most other camps. Because of its relative openness and comprehensiveness in reporting local, national, and international stories, the *Free Press* became the voice of the Nisei in all the camps, circulating by mail to the others.

The *Free Press* carried accurate descriptions of conditions at Manzanar, of the farms, the Cooperative (and elections for its board),

Project Attorney
Bunkichi Hayashi (center)

and personnel and assignments of the director and his staff. The tone of the articles was almost always on the positive side—improvements that had been made, others that were possible. By comparing the "official reports" with the diaries, letters, and post-internment writings of the Nisei one senses that the newspaper was censored by its own staff, and simply avoided writing those articles that would cause the director to step in or suspend publication.

FUMIKO HARATA (RIGHT) AND
MRS. MATSUMOTO

The *Free Press* was expressly forbidden to treat only one subject, i.e., any direct criticism of the policy of rounding up and interning the Nisei. The newspaper was, however, allowed to print short, factual stories on the progress through the courts of the various legal challenges to the legality and legitimacy of that policy.

There were four such challenges, but the most important was *Korematsu* v. *the United States*. The *Manzanar Free Press* reported on the loss of that case in the Ninth Circuit Court of Appeals on January 5, 1944, shortly after the decision had been handed down. On February 16, in a dispatch datelined Washington, the *Free Press* reported Fred Korematsu's decision to ask the Supreme Court to accept his case, and review the denial of relief by the Ninth Circuit.

Obviously, the reporters for the newspaper could not leave Manzanar to follow a story. Instead, they gathered "out of town" news from newspapers and letters that arrived in camp by mail—the first Korematsu story came from the *Heart Mountain Sentinel*. The post office became the Nisei equivalent of news agencies like the Associated Press and United Press International, just as it had been for Ben Franklin and other early American printers and publishers.

By the time the Korematsu case was lost in the Supreme Court, in December 1944, the city of Manzanar was gradually disappearing. Almost half its population had been released.

The final judicial approval of the evacuation of the Nisei, as established by *Korematsu*, was reported in the *Free Press*. But on the same day, the Supreme Court handed down the decision in the Endo case, ruling that any Nisei whose loyalty was not questioned could return to his or her place of residence on the West Coast. This decision, which struck down the central premise of the policy of General John L. DeWitt, commander, Western Defense Command, did more than anything else to hasten the resettlement of the people of Manzanar, and the closing of the city in the desert.

The United States Court in Los Angeles . . . has granted a writ of habeas corpus in behalf of a nisei and his wife, permitting their case to be heard. . . .

The very fact that the United States Court consents to hear the case in time of war may be accepted as a sign that our government intends to safeguard our rights. In the face of the periodic public outcries against the evacuees, an unavoidable expression under the circumstances, it is reassuring to know that the calm and just acts of the government go on unperturbed. *[Emphasis in original.]*
FEBRUARY 6, 1943 MANZANAR FREE PRESS

Enemies of the Nation?

The assumption that caused all of the Nisei living on the West Coast to be put in prison camps was that each of them was a potential enemy of the nation. The following three stories represent the range of people taken up in this dragnet, from the very young to the very old.

The stories of this Cub Scout who would become a congressman, this young woman who would become a doctor, and this disabled veteran of the U.S. Navy are taken from testimony before various congressional or Commission hearings, or from the records of Manzanar itself. These people are unique, but their stories are similar to those of the 120,000, some silenced by death, who were in all the camps.

Congressman Norman Mineta of California was a young boy at the time of internment. His father sold insurance in San Jose, his mother was a housewife. Though both had lived in the United States most of their adult lives, they were not citizens because the laws did not allow them to apply.

His three sisters, Etsu, Aya, and Helen, and he and his brother Al, however, were all American citizens. His brother was a premed stu-

Tom Kobayashi

dent at San Jose State. It was clear that none of his family posed any threat to the United States; yet all of them were forced out of their home in San Jose at gunpoint, and taken into the camps. At this time, Norman Mineta was ten years old, and a Cub Scout.

Dr. Mary Oda was a first-year medical student at the University of California when the Los Angeles evacuations were ordered. The university could do nothing to protect its students, but it did give them early oral exams, so they could complete the year before they were taken away. Her family owned one farm, and leased and worked two others. Their farm equipment and crops were sacrificed at less than 8 percent of value. They stored their personal property on the farm. It was gone when they returned.

Dr. Oda's oldest brother was a dentist. He volunteered for the army, was turned down, and was imprisoned at Gila Bend. Her second brother was a third-year dental student. He was taken into camp and then drafted. Another brother, who was a medical student at Marquette, was allowed to remain in college in Wisconsin. She, her younger brother, two sisters, and parents were moved into an eight-cot room at Manzanar.

There, her older sister suffered a nervous breakdown and was hospitalized. Her younger sister developed bronchial asthma in camp, and died of it at age twenty-six. Her oldest brother suffered an intestinal obstruction, was taken to Los Angeles for surgery, and died there. Her father developed nose and throat cancer, perhaps from the wind and the dust at camp, and died.

Dr. Oda got a job as a physician's assistant at the Manzanar Hospital. She witnessed the death of one of the young men shot by guards in the so-called Manzanar Uprising. When she sought to leave Manzanar in order to complete her medical training, she applied to all the medical schools in the country except those on the West Coast. Every one except the Women's Medical College of Pennsylvania turned her down because they "had military installations on campus." They apparently thought any "resident" of Manzanar must be a security risk to the nation.

Her mother, who had been a schoolteacher and wife of a successful farmer, was reduced after her husband's death to working as a farm laborer. She used the $1,800 the government provided for "restitution" to buy a gravestone for her husband, son, and daughter.

HARRY SUMIDA IN HOSPITAL

Nobuteru Harry Sumida was born in New York City in 1872, and raised by foster parents. He never knew his real parents, and may have been the first Nisei in the United States.

A sailor, in 1891 he enlisted in the navy. He was struck in the leg by shrapnel while serving aboard the USS *Indiana* in the Battle of Santiago Bay, in the Spanish-American War.

In 1901 Sumida married Joanna Schmidt, whose pictures are on the table beside him in the photo Ansel Adams took (see page 139). She died in 1941, not seeing the day in 1942 that her husband was removed from the Santa Anita Sanitarium in Los Angeles, where he was pensioned by the U.S. Navy, and taken directly to the hospital at Manzanar.

In January 1943, the Japanese American Joint Board was formed to advise the WRA on the release of prisoners back into the civilian population. The Joint Board consisted almost entirely of representatives of various military intelligence agencies.

The critical question regarding the release was whether to presume loyalty or disloyalty on the part of the vast majority of the Nisei, who had no record whatsoever for anything done or said about Japan. General DeWitt wanted a presumption of guilt unless innocence was shown—a position antithetical to Anglo-American law, of course, in which innocence is presumed until guilt is proven.

General DeWitt's presumption of the guilt of all Nisei was demonstrated from the beginning. Before any Nisei evacuations had occurred, he asked the Federal Communications Commission to investigate 760 instances of possible illegal radio transmissions to Japanese ships off the coast. The FCC replied that 641 involved no transmissions at all.

Of the remaining 119 cases, 21 were from U.S. Army Stations, 8 from navy stations, 12 from local police stations, 65 from U.S. and foreign commercial stations, and 10 from Japanese stations in Japanese-held territories. The remaining three were short-range transmissions from home phonographs.

The FCC later found that reports of possible illegal signaling from the West Coast did not decrease after the evacuation of the Nisei, and similar levels of false reports applied elsewhere in the country. Still, DeWitt's final report perpetuated his claim that Nisei signaled to Japanese ships in the Pacific.

Roy Takeno (right) and Mayor at Town Hall Meeting

Perhaps the clearest indication of General DeWitt's attitude appeared in the following exchange in a telephone conversation with Assistant Secretary of War John J. McCloy, just before Executive Order 9066 was issued:

"McCloy: You may . . . conceivably permit some [of the Japs] to come back whom you are quite certain are free from any suspicion, as . . . you might let some Italians come back. Now that has a sound legal basis for it.

"DeWitt: . . . you don't have to worry about them [the Germans and the Italians] as a group. You have to worry about them purely as individuals. Out here, Mr. Secretary, a Jap is a Jap to these people now."

The transcript of this call, and other documents contradicting General DeWitt, did not come to light until 1982, through the efforts of the Commission on the Wartime Relocation and Internment of Civilians.

In carrying out Executive Order 9066, General DeWitt repeatedly referred to "Japanese aliens and non-aliens." In hearings before the Commission on Internment, on July 14, 1981, Fred Beck, for the army, sought to explain the logic of General DeWitt's use of this phrase, as the following exchange between Commissioner Marutani and Mr. Beck shows:

"Marutani: . . . What is a non-alien?

"Beck: That was General DeWitt's particular usage.

"Marutani: Yes, but what is a 'non-alien'?

"Beck: A citizen."

The truth of "disloyalty" by the people that General DeWitt called "aliens and non-aliens" was this: In the entire course of the war, ten people in the United States were convicted of spying for Japan. All of them were Caucasians.

When it became clear, in 1943, that the interned citizens would be released, the Joint Board found it did not need to resolve the fundamental question of the presumption of innocence at all. Instead, it looked for "factors" suggesting the *possibility* of disloyalty, including being partially educated in Japan, refusal to register, being an officer in an organization controlled by aliens, or having bank deposits in Japan. None of these actually constituted an act of disloyalty, and many such "factors" also applied to millions of Americans of German or Italian descent, who were not incarcerated.

Even by these criteria, the Joint Board, over the course of a year, recommended the release of more than 25,000 people. It also recommended the continued incarceration of more than 12,600. Despite the Joint Board's recommendation, the WRA released more than six thousand of this second group, and it is worthwhile to note that no acts of sabotage or espionage were ever reported among even this group of "suspect" people.

Abolishing the Joint Board in early 1944, because it was acting too slowly, the WRA adopted a policy of releasing prisoners from camps as quickly as possible. There were two methods of doing so. One was to review and change prior negative information in a file—to "reevaluate" the prisoner positively; another was to grant the prisoner an "indefinite leave." Those on such "indefinite leave" were

[From a letter from Chiye Mori, editor of the Free Press, *to the head of the Resettlement office, printed in the newspaper.] Being in camp I hadn't realized how much I was missing, how it felt to be able to walk down a glittering avenue of shop windows, to hear music floating out of cocktail bars, to feel the surge of a tired crowd, pushing its way home. It's really wonderful to feel again the pulse of a big city. And the people here are so friendly, more so than I ever thought they would be. They take you for granted; they don't even look at you, and what a swell feeling that is, after the dirty looks we got in California.*
JUNE 2, 1943 MANZANAR FREE PRESS

CHOIR GROUP

never expected to return to the camps. Technically, however, they were still in the custody or jurisdiction of the WRA. Against widespread popular opposition to the release of the Nisei, the WRA, under the leadership of its last director, Dillon Myer, was hoping that the Supreme Court would issue a definitive ruling to end the internments.

Instead, the Supreme Court's decision accepted the entire internment process as constitutional and left the stamp of potential disloyalty on all Nisei.

Younger attorneys for the Department of Justice, asked to defend the President's Order, realized it was based almost entirely on De-Witt's final report. They knew the navy, the FBI, the FCC, and even army intelligence contradicted DeWitt. They concluded, "There is no doubt that [DeWitt's] statements are intentional falsehoods." And, "we . . . [may] have a duty to advise the Court of the Ringle memorandum. . . . Any other course of conduct might approximate the suppression of evidence." They suggested a footnote in the brief to warn the Court that the final report was inaccurate. Senior officials of the War and Justice departments overruled the idea. The Court was not warned.

Five members of the Court concluded that Executive Order 9066 was within the constitutional powers of the President.

They said, "It was because we could not reject the finding of the military authorities that it was impossible to bring about an immediate segregation of the disloyal from the loyal that we sustained the validity of the curfew order as applied to the whole group." On the same basis, without examining General DeWitt's assertions, the Court upheld the exclusions also.

Justice Frankfurter concurred: "The validity of the action under the war power must be judged wholly in the context of war." (This distinction was abandoned in a case during the Korean War.)

Three justices understood what General DeWitt was doing and why. They saw that Executive Order 9066 posed a continuing threat to any group of any type.

Justice Roberts said, " . . . [This] is the case of convicting a citizen as a punishment for not submitting to imprisonment in a concentration camp, based on his ancestry . . . without evidence or inquiry concerning his loyalty . . . towards the United States."

Justice Murphy got directly to the point: "Such exclusion goes over the 'very brink of constitutional power,' and falls into the ugly abyss of racism."

In his dissent, Justice Jackson described the continuing danger of the decision: "A military order, however unconstitutional, is not apt to last longer than the military emergency. . . . But once a judicial opinion rationalizes such an order . . . the Court for all time has validated the principle of racial discrimination. . . . The principle then lies about like a loaded weapon ready for the hand of any authority that can bring forward a plausible claim of an urgent need. . . . Nothing better illustrates the danger than does the Court's opinion in this case."

On April 19, 1984, forty years later, United States District Court Judge June Patel, in California, vacated the conviction of Fred Korematsu. She concluded, "Korematsu . . . stands as a caution that in

times of international hostility . . . our institutions, legislative, executive and judicial, must be prepared to exercise their authority to protect all citizens from petty fears and prejudices that are so easily aroused."

Dr. Oda, Representative Mineta, Harry Sumida, and all the others remain to this day accused of—but never charged with, or convicted of—disloyalty to the United States. In the eyes of the American system of justice, they remained potential enemies of the nation.

In Service of Their Country

軍隊

Roy Takeno, editor of the *Manzanar Free Press,* said in his New Year's Day editorial that it was important to the Nisei to prove themselves to their countrymen. The surest way to do so, and the first method by which many of them got out of the camps, was by joining the military.

The decision to allow Nisei to serve in the army was heavily debated within the administration. General DeWitt fought the idea strenuously. But he was not to prevail, and the new policy was announced by President Roosevelt in February 1943. "The principle on which this country was founded and by which it has always been governed is that Americanism is a matter of the mind and heart; Americanism is not, and never was, a matter of race or ancestry. . . . Every loyal American should be given the opportunity to serve this country wherever his skills will make the greatest contribution— whether it be in the ranks of our armed forces, war production, agriculture, government service, or other work essential to the war effort."

The very existence of the camps, of course, contradicted his words. Still, his statement meant that the Nisei could serve in the American army. Thousands volunteered, and thousands more registered for the draft. With that decision, the gates of Manzanar and the other camps cracked open just a bit.

CORPORAL JIMMIE SHOHARA'S RIBBONS

Yet even in the army, the Nisei who served in World War II faced difficulties much like those of their parents, brothers, and sisters in the camps. Because of doubts about its loyalty, the 100th Infantry Battalion of the Hawaii National Guard, for example, was transferred to the mainland, to Camp McCoy, Wisconsin—and then was given only wooden guns to train with. The army read all the letters they sent home. Senator Spark Matsunaga, who was in that unit, wrote, "We learned subsequently that because of the tenor of our letters the War Department decided to give us a chance. [When] our guns were returned to us and we . . . prepared for combat duty—grown men leaped with joy."

The 100th Battalion was united with the 442nd Regimental Combat Team at Camp Shelby, Mississippi. The 442nd was composed of Nisei who had volunteered and been drafted from inside the prison camps. Both units fought with great distinction in Italy and France, and were responsible for the rescue of the "Lost Battalion" of the 36th Texas Division.

In seven major campaigns, the combined 100th and 442nd suffered 9,486 casualties and won 18,143 individual decorations for valor in battle, including one Congressional Medal of Honor and almost ten thousand Purple Hearts.

The casualty rate in the "Nisei Regiment" was more than 300 percent of its authorized strength of four thousand men. Man for man, no American fighting unit in any war this nation has ever fought took greater casualties or earned more commendations than this regiment. Those who fought alongside them, those who owe their lives to the

Corporal Jimmie Shohara

skills of the 442nd, were unanimous in their praise of the courage and skill of these Nisei.

The 442nd was also known as the "Christmas Tree Regiment" because of its many decorations. The last honor it earned was a Presidential Unit Banner, which President Truman affixed to the colors of the 442nd on July 15, 1946. He told those veterans present for the ceremony, "You fought, not only the enemy, but prejudice—and you won."

But not only men served, of course. Nisei women volunteered for the WACs, and as army nurses, and for the Red Cross. They, too, served with great distinction. They, too, suffered casualties.

But the least-known service of this group to the American war effort was in the South Pacific. More than sixteen thousand Nisei served in the Pacific and in Asia. Most served in military intelligence with the army as it fought its way from the Philippines up the islands to Iwo Jima and beyond, translating captured documents and intercepted radio messages.

While the Caucasian officers were commissioned, Nisei intelligence officers were given noncommissioned ranks. Still, the value of the Nisei in the Military Intelligence Service (MIS) was such that in the field they were usually assigned several regular soldiers to guard against their being mistaken for the enemy by other American troops.

Still other Nisei went behind Japanese lines. Their contribution was especially valuable to the war effort—but also especially dangerous. Those who were captured were not always held as prisoners of war—they were often summarily shot.

Private Kato

Private Margaret Fukuoka, WAC

Nearly 300 stars will grace Manzanar's Service flag to honor those who are full-fledged nephews of Uncle Sam. Each star will represent one serviceman from this center, including all soldiers with families in Manzanar.

April 7, 1943 Manzanar Free Press

In all, more than 33,000 Nisei served in the American army in World War II, a remarkably high number, since the total population of Nisei, both on the mainland and in Hawaii, was just 278,000. No similar group in the United States demonstrated greater dedication, skill, or sacrifice in the war effort than this one.

Despite this, some in the military continued to attack Nisei abilities and commitment, though these attacks were sometimes challenged, as the following exchange shows. A certain Navy Commander Wassell, at a War Loan Drive in Los Angeles, had been quoted by the *San Francisco Chronicle*, in June 1944, as saying "The grandest thing that was done in the United States was done when General DeWitt put all the Japanese in California under barbed wire. No doubt there are some Japanese in the U.S. who are just as loyal as I am but I defy any group of men and women to separate the chaff from the grain. It can't be done."

On learning this, Secretary Ickes promptly contacted Commander Wassell's superior, Secretary of the Navy James Forrestal, commenting, "I am sure that you appreciate how immeasurably such a comment . . . has increased the burden . . . of resettling loyal citizens and law-abiding aliens of Japanese descent. I would appreciate . . . any comments that you may have regarding Commander Wassell's authority to make such remarks in public."

Ickes himself received a very different sort of letter, and it, and his reply, were both issued to the public by the Interior Department in a press release. Army Corporal J. H. Kety had written from Italy, "May I suggest that you send all those narrow-minded, bigoted, un-Americans over here to relieve the 100th Battalion? Out of . . . 1,000 men, 900 have . . . Purple Hearts . . . 36 have . . . the Silver Star; 21 have won Bronze Stars, and 3 wear the Distinguished Service Cross."

Secretary Ickes's reply to Corporal Kety read, in part, "Thank you for your letter. It is quite apparent that you know what you are fighting for."

Elsewhere, General Woodbury Willoughby, chief of intelligence for General MacArthur, reported that the work of the Nisei Military Intelligence Service had shortened the war in the Pacific by up to two years. Among that group's individual achievements were the translation of documents from Guadalcanal, providing a complete listing of the Imperial Japanese Navy's ships, and its air squadrons and bases. Another was the translation of Japan's entire battle plan for the defense of the Philippines. But the work of the intelligence specialists remained unknown to the public until long after the war.

The motto of the 442nd was "Go for Broke." On June 17, 1987, Mike Masaoka, head of the Go For Broke Nisei Veterans Association, testified to a Senate committee that "[we] pay our special respects and tribute to our fellow American Japanese in the Pacific . . . and in . . . China, Burma, India. . . . Since most [of their activities] . . . still remain classified 'secret,' they did not receive the publicity or plaudits they so richly deserved. Still, in my . . . opinion . . . shared by most . . . in the 442nd, they contributed far more to the ultimate surrender of the Japanese militarists than we did to the Allied victory in Europe."

Infantryman Harry Takagi explained what the Nisei were fighting for: "We were fighting for the rights of all Japanese Americans. We set out to break every record in the army. If we failed, it would reflect discredit on all Japanese Americans. We could not let that happen."

A LEGACY OF SHAME

Forty percent of the survivors of the Issei, those Japanese who entered the United States prior to 1924 but were never permitted to apply for citizenship, and who were interned at Manzanar and other camps, now live in the greater Los Angeles area. One-fifth of them live below the poverty level. Most have problems with health care, housing, and access to government services. Yet before they were interned, almost all were members of cohesive, self-sufficient families.

Precedents exist for monetary settlements to Americans who have been denied their constitutional rights by actions of the federal government. In September 1978, the American Indian Commission awarded $800 million to Native Americans covering more than five hundred claims relating to treaties that had been breached by the government. In December 1980, the government paid ten thousand dollars to each of 1,318 anti–Vietnam War demonstrators who had been imprisoned wrongfully for a weekend. In 1986, Congress set a figure of fifty dollars per day as recompense for Americans held hostage abroad, and paid $22,200 apiece to the fifty-two Americans held hostage by Iran for 444 days.

It is ironic to mention generations of Indian treaties broken, or the loss of all possessions and years of imprisonment that the Nisei

MANZANAR FROM GUARD TOWER:
SUMMER HEAT

suffered, or the Iranian hostages, in the same breath as a weekend of incarceration by protesters. However, the fact that the government paid so much for so little makes it clear that the present proposed law to pay twenty thousand dollars to each of the surviving Nisei who were imprisoned in internment camps is certainly not an unreasonable demand; if anything, it represents the minimal amount deserved.

One earlier effort was made to compensate the Nisei. The Japanese American Evacuation Claims Act of 1948 applied only to property losses, required elaborate documentation, and ultimately paid only $37 million against $148 million in claims. Also, it paid in 1942 dollars and without interest. It offered nothing to account for the strain of imprisonment itself, for lost income, or even for some major categories of property, such as crops left in the fields as the Nisei were taken away.

CHILDREN AT SUNDAY SCHOOL CLASS

In 1951, Congress modified the act to allow summary payment of claims less than $2,500. In desperation, many of the Nisei abandoned part of their claimed losses just to get prompt payment. Congress made a final amendment to the act in 1965, allowing summary settlement of remaining claims up to $100,000.

The net result of the 1948 act was that less than 10 percent was paid of some of the property losses on 26,568 claims. Throughout its application, the procedures used and the amounts paid were both inadequate, and the act did little or nothing for a majority of the Nisei. Congress at the time was given to referring to the act as the "pots and pans bill."

Senate Bill 1009 and its companion bill in the House, H. 442, outline the present proposal for restitution and apology. On September 17, 1987, the bill passed the House. On April 20, 1988, S. 1009 passed the Senate, and the differing bills went to conference committee. The final bill was signed by the President on August 10, 1988.

The restitution act provides compensation only for those inmates who have survived for forty-seven years to receive it. One-half of those who were imprisoned, 60,000 people, died before this apology was made and restitution offered. In memory of these people, and for their families, the act offers nothing. The legal case seeking court-ordered restitution will continue on their behalf.

S. 1009 provides for the following: an apology for the internment of the Nisei; review of convictions and pardons for those convicted of "crimes" relating to noncooperation with the various evacuation orders; payment of $20,000 to each individual who was imprisoned under Executive Order 9066, and the establishment of the Civil Liberties Public Education Fund and a board to administer it.

(S. 1009 also establishes the Aleutian and Pribilof Islands Restitution Fund, and makes various provisions for the former residents of Aleut and Attu. The Aleut Indians were evacuated by the U.S. Navy after the Japanese invaded the Aleutian Islands. Although there was a clear military need to get them out of the war zone, they were placed in deplorable camps in Alaska, where more than 10 percent of them died before the war's end.)

The record of the courts in providing redress to the Nisei has been worse than that of Congress. The criminal records of those convicted of failing to obey the Evacuation Orders have been expunged; but beyond that, *Korematsu* still stands as valid law, holding the internments constitutional.

The last case to date, a class action named *Hohri* v. *the United States*, was filed in March 1983, and seeks damages from the government for civil rights violations. The plaintiffs claimed that the case could be brought now, because only since 1980 had documents come to light that showed the "intentional falsity" of the government's case in 1943. In May 1984, however, the trial court dismissed the case as "untimely."

Then, in June 1987, the Supreme Court ruled 8–0 that the case should have been appealed through the U.S. Court of Appeals for the Federal Circuit, and sent the case there for further proceedings. The Supreme Court made no comment on the merits of the case, and no comment on its own decision in *Korematsu*, forty-three years before. As of 1988, at least two years of litigation lay ahead before the Hohri case would reach a final decision in the Supreme Court. The case continues in appeals, but meanwhile no judge has yet awarded any damages.

As the case continues, year after year, and as restitution is delayed up to four years, more and more of the Nisei die without receiving justice from their country.

At present, the official position of the government on the internment was expressed on June 17, 1987, by Richard K. Willard,

PHILIP HARA, IN CHARGE OF WORK-OFFER SIGNS

Assistant Attorney General, before the Senate Committee on Governmental Affairs. He said, "We question the wisdom, and indeed the propriety, of accusing leaders of the United States government during World War II, both civilian and military, of dishonorable behavior. ... These matters are best left to historical and scholarly analysis rather than debated by Congress."

Ansel Adams took photographs of Manzanar to make a permanent record of an injustice committed by the government, and of the people who suffered for it. He gave them to the Library of Congress so the story would always be on public record. The newly declassified documents and testimony from witnesses at Manzanar and elsewhere confirm the truth of what he said then, and what we are beginning to understand now.

The events and facts in this book paint a harsh picture of the United States. All three branches of our government—Executive, Legislative, and Judicial—engaged in a massive violation of the constitutional rights of American citizens. But forty-five years later, the Constitution is reasserting itself. The President and the Congress have righted their wrongs. Only the reversal of *Korematsu*, the apology by the Supreme Court, remains to be accomplished.

Few nations possess the constitutional guarantees that the United States enjoys. Fewer still engage in the unending and difficult task of living by such guarantees. In the United States we have set ourselves a higher standard. And by that standard, the shame of this nation for its treatment of the Nisei is not yet over.

Memories of Manzanar

The memories of Manzanar come in two forms. One is the words of people who were there, such as Dr. Mary Oda and soldier Arnold Yoshizawa, who have testified in public hearings nearly half a century later about their experiences, which are still fresh in their minds, and cruel.

The other memory is an institutional one. It is history found in ancient documents and in modern findings. It includes the possibility that this might happen again, but only if we are careless, only if we forget what happened once.

Dr. Oda, a medical student in 1942, described Manzanar in these words:

> After living in a comfortable, four-bedroom house, the cramped, eight-cot room was stifling. We shared the room with an elderly couple in their eighties, a Christian minister and his wife. The room had no inner wall, [just] open studs exposing two-by-fours. . . . The floor was wooden, with half-inch gaps between the planks where you could see the earth below and through which the winds blew up layers of sand and dust everywhere.
>
> We slept on straw which we stuffed into bags—that was our first chore upon arrival in camp. Later my little brother

BIRDS ON WIRE, EVENING

made makeshift chairs and a table from a pile of scrap lumber. Several months later linoleum was laid down, cutting down the thickness of the dust that settled after the winds blew, which was often.

The bathroom was communal, with no partitions between the toilet seats, which numbered about a dozen. The shower was also communal. There was a total lack of privacy for such basic intimate functions.

We left for camp at a bus stop in Burbank on a gray, cloudy day. . . . It began to rain. A mother of two, standing next to me, said, 'See, even God in heaven is crying for us.' At the time I felt numb and bewildered by what was happening, but today, when I remember this, the tears come readily. The trip was long, the landscape barren and desolate. My first reaction to camp was one of dismay and disbelief. . . . The newspapers had reported that we were to be placed in comfortable homes. Our new home looked exactly like a prison camp—the barbed wire, watchtowers, military police with guns, [that] you all know about.

Arnold Yoshizawa was a boy, living with his family in Los Angeles in the early 1940s. He wrote:

On the night of December 7, 1941, my father was arrested by three FBI agents and taken to the L.A. County Jail. . . . [Ultimately] he was transferred . . . to Fort Missoula, Montana. He was guilty of no crime. . . .

[After] passage of Executive Order 9066 . . . [we were forced] to liquidate all [our] belongings and prepare to be

[From highlights of 1942.] The first baby born was a boy . . . Kenji Ogawa, on April 16. . . . The [first] marriage [was] Kimiko Wakamura [and] Howard Kumagai . . . on April 20. . . . [The] first death reported was that of Matsunosuke Murakami, 62, on May 16.
JANUARY 6, 1943 MANZANAR FREE PRESS

evacuated within a very short time. All household and family belongings were either given away or sold at ridiculous prices as non-Japanese carpetbaggers took advantage of us, offering five dollars for our refrigerator, two dollars for our stove, one dollar for our bed and mattress, etc.

After our house was nearly emptied of all these cherished mementos, we packed our personal belongings, only [as much as] we could hand-carry, into suitcases, and moved to a small hotel near the railroad station a few days before we were to be forcibly evacuated to Manzanar under armed guard.

Because there was no espionage or spying evidence against him, my father, after five and a half months, was released to his home in Boyle Heights, but, to his dismay, found his family gone. Luckily, the day before we were to be evacuated, he found us at the hotel. . . .

During World War II, I was too young to enter military service; however, after graduating from high school, I enlisted in the U.S. Army and was stationed in Japan. At the outbreak of the Korean War . . . I volunteered for combat duty, as I felt it was my duty for my family's honor. I remember the day I returned home, how proud my father was that I had served the United States of America. . . .

While fighting and being cleared for handling top secret material during the Korean War, how ironic that on the security questionnaire I had to list my father and uncle as my enemy. It would be years later that they would be dropped from the parole status. They both died a few years ago, not realizing redress or apology due them.

During the war, the Western Defense Command passed from General DeWitt to Lt. Gen. Delos Emmons. Emmons had become the commanding general on Hawaii, after Pearl Harbor. He had successfully resisted the internment of all Nisei on Hawaii.

The experience of Hawaii stands in sharp contrast to that of the West Coast. There were almost 158,000 Nisei on Hawaii in December 1941. They constituted more than 35 percent of the population and a significant proportion of the armed forces and the civilian employees of the army and navy.

Martial law was declared on Hawaii in joint actions by the territorial governor and General Emmons, commander of the Hawaiian Department. In his first radio address on December 21, 1941, General Emmons said:

> . . . there is no intention or desire on the part of the federal authorities to operate mass concentration camps. No person, be he citizen or alien, need worry, provided he is not connected with subversive elements. . . .
>
> While we have been subjected to a serious attack by a ruthless and treacherous enemy, we must remember that this is America and we must do things the American way. We must distinguish between loyalty and disloyalty among our people.

General Emmons was under constant pressure from his superiors to arrange for mass deportation of the Hawaiian Nisei, either to the mainland, or to camps to be built on one of the smaller islands. He deflected the pressure by practical means.

PICTURES AND MEMENTOS

Emmons noted that he lacked the shipping to transport more than 100,000 Nisei to the mainland. He lacked the materials and the manpower to build or guard camps on Hawaii for this many people. He noted that 90 percent of the carpenters on Hawaii were Nisei, and they were needed to rebuild after Pearl Harbor. He noted that there were 20,000 white women and children who wanted to get back to the mainland but could not. He noted the chronic shortages of war materials on the islands, which took priority over materials to build camps. And he constantly fought against false and inflammatory information.

Angus Taylor, acting United States attorney for Hawaii, prepared a report to the War Department urging internment of all Nisei in Hawaii. General Emmons's reply was in a letter of March 29, 1942, to Assistant Secretary McCloy:

> The feeling that invasion is imminent is not the belief of most of the responsible people. . . . There have been no acts of sabotage committed in Hawaii.
>
> I talked with Mr. Taylor . . . [about] evidence of subversive or disloyal acts. . . . Since that time he has . . . furnished information about individuals and groups which turned out to be based on rumor or imagination. He has furnished absolutely no information of value.
>
> Mr. Taylor is a conscientious, but highly emotional, violently anti-Japanese lawyer who distrusts the FBI, Naval Intelligence and the Army Intelligence. . . . I do not believe he is sufficiently informed on the Japanese question to express an official opinion.

Despite communications from Secretary of War Stimson and President Roosevelt, General Emmons held to his position. On April 2, 1943, the War Department finally ordered General Emmons to suspend evacuations to the mainland. Fewer than two thousand Nisei, each of whom had been sent for individual reasons, were interned from Hawaii.

General Emmons's approach had proved correct: no Nisei in Hawaii were ever convicted of any crime of spying or espionage.

Still, in January 1947, long after the war was over, the WDC issued its recommendations for handling suspect civilian populations in the next war. The report attacked the court system as the means for determining guilt or innocence. It said, "Many people . . . would be quite undisturbed by the fact that possibly some who should have been goats were labeled as sheep. It is a real question whether in wartime we can afford to protect our peace and security by these quite slipshod determinations."

On the subject of trial by jury, the WDC said, "The theory that any reasonably honest and intelligent person is capable of passing judgment upon many complex factors is certainly open to severe question in the case of making determinations in the interest of the peace and security of the country in time of war."

Instead of letting courts and juries determine guilt or innocence on such matters, the WDC recommended that in the future such matters be left to a special military unit. It also recommended the establishment of a "citizen education program," to prepare the people to accept such a process, should another war break out.

The suggestion that the Western Defense Command would purposely repeat its mistakes from World War II in the next war is perhaps Manzanar's grimmest legacy. We would do better to remember the lives and the faces of the Nisei in the camps as expressed in the photographs of Ansel Adams, to learn from these harsh events, and, having learned, never repeat them.

恥辱　SHAME　*CHIZOKU*

追想　RECOLLECTION　*TSUISO*

文化　CULTURE　*BUNKA*

新聞　NEWSPAPER　*SHIMBUN*

圧迫　OPPRESSION　*APPAKU*

出所　RETURN　*SHUSHOKU*

軍隊　MILITARY　*GUNTAI*

A Translation of the Japanese Calligraphy

 MANZANAR *RINGO-EN*

 CONTENTS *MOKUJI*

 MISTAKE *MACHIGAI*

NISEI *NISEI*

 EVACUATE *TACHINOKI*

 HUT *KOYA*

 FARM *NOJO*

 STORE *TENPO*

PROFESSION *SENGYO*

 EDUCATION *KYOIKU*